OSPREY
PUBLISHING

Armored Units of the Russian Civil War

White and Allied

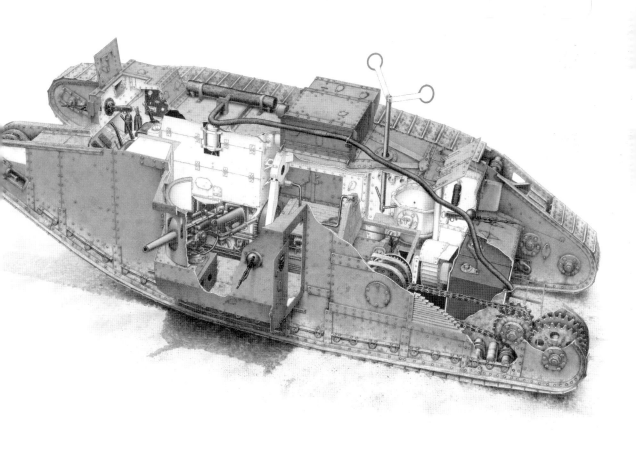

D Bullock & A Deryabin • Illustrated by A Aksenov

First published in Great Britain in 2003 by Osprey Publishing, Elms Court, Chapel Way, Botley, Oxford OX2 9LP, United Kingdom.
Email: info@ospreypublishing.com

A CIP catalogue record for this book is available from the British Library.

ISBN 1 84176 544 9

Editor: Simone Drinkwater
Design: Melissa Orrom Swan
Index by David Worthington
Originated by Grasmere Digital Imaging, Leeds, UK
Printed in China through World Print Ltd.

05 06 07 08   10 9 8 7 6 5 4 3 2

FOR A CATALOGUE OF ALL BOOKS PUBLISHED BY OSPREY PLEASE CONTACT:

NORTH AMERICA
Osprey Direct, 2427 Bond Street,
University Park, IL 60466, USA
E-mail: info@ospreydirectusa.com

ALL OTHER REGIONS
Osprey Direct UK, P.O. Box 140,
Wellingborough, Northants, NN8 2FA, UK
E-mail: info@ospreydirect.co.uk

www.ospreypublishing.com

Authors' acknowledgements

We would like to thank Maxim Kolomiets who contributed several photographs, as well as the following Russian historians: Sergei Volkov, Michael Blinov, Alexander Voronov, Timur Jalilov, Sergei Gnedin, Sergei Ivanikov, Vladimir Lobytsyn, Maria Maltseva and Vladimir Peredery.

David Bullock's acknowledgements

I would like to thank my parents for financial support that made my trips to Russia and the Ukraine possible. Major Clint Markusch, USAF (ret.) sacrificed many evenings photocopying and Sergei Drobiazko assisted with vital communications in Moscow. David Fletcher of the Tank Museum provided professional and courteous assistance. Major Craig Martelle, USMC, (ret.) provided vital contacts while serving at the American Embassy in Moscow. Major Tom Hillman, USA, greatly assisted with translations and offered real partnership while helping solve several important questions.

Author's note

We have examined White and Allied armor. For the most part, we have not examined the armor of the newly emergent nations that were neither White nor allied to the Whites. There is a 13-day difference between the Gregorian calendar used in the West (and by the Reds after the Revolution) and the older Julian calendar which is referenced in many White Army archives, especially in the southern theater. For example, according to the Gregorian calendar, the "October Revolution" of 1917 actually took place in November 1917. We have attempted to ensure that dates given in this book follow the Gregorian calendar. Most armored fighting vehicles had names and we have tried to translate those of them that "make sense" into English, whilst transliterating those that might not. We have not adopted a strict methodology when spelling names and geographical locations; rather, we have tried to go with spellings most comprehensible to a Western audience. This book is the first of a two-part series. The words "division" and "divizion" in the text should not be confused. Translated from Russian, "divizion" means two or more armored car or tank detachments, or two or more batteries (each armored train equaling a battery).

Artist's note

Readers may care to note that the original paintings from which the color plates in this book were prepared are available for private sale. All reproduction copyright whatsoever is retained by the Publishers. All enquiries should be addressed to:

Andrei Yurievich Aksenov, Moldagulovoy Street 10, Korpus 3, Kvartira 78, Moscow, 111395 Russia

The Publishers regret that they can enter into no correspondence upon this matter.

ARMORED UNITS OF THE RUSSIAN CIVIL WAR: WHITE AND ALLIED

INTRODUCTION

Armored cars *Zhorki*, ("Vigilant"), *Smelyi*, ("Brave") and *Moguchi*, ("Mighty"), 2nd Armored Car Detachment, 2nd Armored Car Divizion, General Baron Peter Wrangel's Caucasian Army, Armed Forces of South Russia. All vehicles were Russian Austin third production series dispatched from Great Britain and disembarked on 25 April 1919 in the port of Novorossisk. Each flies the Russian national tricolor flag of blue, red and white and bears the Volunteer Army chevron on the armored doors in the same colors. Originally adopted by the Volunteer Army, the chevron often appeared by early February 1919 in all armies subordinate to the Armed Forces of South Russia, commanded by General Anton Ivanovich Denikin. Vehicle names were in white below the turrets. (Deryabin)

The number of tanks, armored trains and armored cars that participated in the Russian Civil War on all fronts, including all nationalities, certainly totaled less than 1,000 and probably not much more than 700. Insignificant by the standards of World War II, these armored units nevertheless exerted an influence disproportionate to their actual numbers on the battlefields of what would become the most important civil war of the 20th century. Wherever terrain permitted and whenever assets were available operationally, armored units spearheaded the major offensives, primarily along the railways that were the main arteries of advance for all combatant forces.

Gone were the static trench lines of World War I. This was a new kind of war, capitalizing on mobility and shock. Once again, cavalry emerged to threaten flanks and rear and to deliver the age-old frontal charge of the *arme blanche*. Soldiers hastily conscripted by one political faction, and then by another, often wavered or melted away *en masse*. Elite units with high morale dominated the immense landscapes of the former Russian Empire and advances were counted not in yards, but in hundreds of miles. With no firm front lines and with rear areas frequently left unsecured, partisans, nationalists and brigands, variously hewing to the political colors of Red, White, Green and Black, ravaged towns and countryside.

In this maelstrom, the new instruments of war, the armored units, flourished.

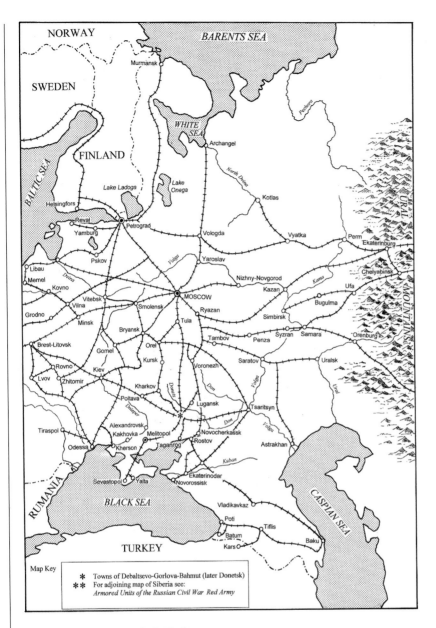

Map Key

* Towns of Debaltsevo-Gorlova-Bahmut (later Donetsk)
** For adjoining map of Siberia see:
Armored Units of the Russian Civil War Red Army

ARMORED CARS

Before the red dawn of the Bolshevik October Revolution of 1917, only one other nation, Great Britain, possessed more armored cars than did Russia. The Russian Ministry of Defense had established its first armored car formation, the 1st Armored Automobile Company, on 19 August 1914, shortly after the outbreak of World War I. By the end of summer 1917, the Russians had produced at least 201 armored cars and had imported over 346 cars or chassis, mostly from Britain, France, the United States and Italy.

Most of these had fallen into the hands of the new Red Army by the end of 1917. Consequently, the White armies that began forming in the Kuban, the Don, in the north and along the Volga, either had to create makeshift armored cars, wait for Allied aid to arrive, or seize them from their Red opponents.

Don Cossack armored car *Ataman Bogaevsky*, Austin, third production series, in Rostov-on-Don, 1919. The car was named for the Cossack host leader who succeeded Ataman Krasnov early in 1919. General A.P. Bogaevsky fought alongside the Volunteer Army from the first campaign in the Kuban and remained, faithfully, to the last. His name appears in white below the turret and beneath that is the black triangle with black border and yellow field insignia of the Don Cossacks, which they painted on their armored cars, trains and aircraft. The Russian colors of blue, red and white are on the roundel in front and demonstrate the Don Cossacks' subordination to the Armed Forces of South Russia under General Denikin. A white stripe is to the rear. One searchlight is atop the turret opposite the driver. (Deryabin)

White Army orders of battle and memoirs of the 1918–22 period record many makes and variants of armored cars. Additionally, there were almost as many smaller modifications as the number of cars themselves, a fact dictated by local needs and creativity, lack of parts, battle damage and a lack of centralized coordination between the fronts. Most of the cars imported by the Whites during the Civil War came from Britain. There seems to have been no factory under White jurisdiction that specifically produced armored cars. Armored cars were repaired or modified according to local capabilities behind the disparate fronts.

Armored cars in the White armies included the Austin first, second and third series, each with Russian modifications made during World War I (described below), and several Russian makes that included:

Russo-Balt (Ten made in 1914, three 7.62mm Maxim machine guns)

Jeffrey-Poplavko (31 made in 1916, two 7.62mm machine guns)

Filiatov (Ten made in 1916 with two 7.62mm machine guns, 20 with only one)

Garford-Putilov and Garford-Putilov Navy (48 made in 1915–16, one 76mm gun, three 7.62mm Maxim machine guns)

Packard (31 made in 1916, one auto 37mm gun)

Fiat-Izhorski (47 made in 1917, two 7.62mm machine guns)

Russia also had access to numbers of Lanchester, Benz, White, Peerless, Pierce-Arrow Naval, Armstrong-Whitworth-Fiat, Armstrong-Whitworth-Jeffries and Fibra armored cars. Only a handful of each make (except for the Austin series described below) could be found distributed amongst the various White forces scattered throughout the former Russian Empire. For this reason, a more thorough examination of Russia's production in World War I and subsequent Red capability will be given in the second part of this series, *Armored Units of the Russian Civil War Red Army*.

The best and most numerous armored car in the White inventory was the Austin, especially the modified second and third series. In September 1914, the Russians had asked the Austin Motor Company Ltd., based in Birmingham, England, to build 48 armored cars with two turrets each carrying a single machine gun that could engage two targets simultaneously. The result was the 30-hp, rear axle driven Austin first series, Model 1914. After being tested in combat, however, the Russians had to completely refit the vehicles with thicker 7mm (0.28in.) plate armor at the Izhorski Works.

The British-produced Austin second series, Model 1915, began arriving in Russia in August 1915. This variant maintained side-by-side turrets, but had a stronger 1.5-ton truck chassis, 50-hp engine and thicker 8mm (0.31in.) armor (probably only 5mm/0.20in. on top); the same armor also featured on the third series. The roof above the driver had been slanted to allow better visibility, but the rear exit door had been removed. The Russians modified these 60 armored cars by adding machine-gun shields, a rear access door and by constructing a rear driver's post, allowing the vehicle to be driven backwards. All British-produced Austin series sent to Russia had a left driver's side door. All series modified inside Russia had two 7.62mm Maxim water-cooled machine guns and preferably carried 6,000 rounds.

Subsequently, the Russians ordered 60 Austin third series, Model 1916, armored cars and these arrived in the spring and summer of 1917. The third series featured diagonally positioned turrets that allowed for a slimmer hull, and had been fitted with bulletproof glass in the front driver position. The second and third series Austin could attain speeds of 30–38mph (50–60km/hr) and carried a crew of five: two drivers (front and rear), two machine-gunners and a commander.

From 1916, most armored cars, including the Austin, had been manufactured or modified with pneumatic tires filled with a special bulletproof mass. Theoretically, all armored cars had felt-lined interiors to protect the crew against metal splinters. There were two other Austin variants, the "Russian Austin" and the Austin-Kegresse half-track, but these were manufactured under the auspices of the Red Army and were only available to the Whites as prizes of war.

On the battlefield, armored cars made their greatest contribution in psychological terms. Their arrival could cause panic in the enemy cavalry and infantry and immediately improve friendly morale, similar to the arrival of armored knights amidst foot soldiers in earlier centuries. In this new civil war of shock and mobility, armored cars maneuvered and emitted high rates of machine-gun fire at close distances. Opponents had to rely on their own artillery to drive the steel intruders from the field.

Moreover, armored cars frequently supported the advance of the numerous and often elite White cavalry, particularly in the southern theater which had relatively solid and flat terrain. They could maneuver and anchor flanks or punch frontally, thereby multiplying the shock effect of the cavalry. Their turrets could rotate in nearly all directions, making them a superior fire platform to the famous tachanka, or Maxim machine-gun cart used by all sides, but especially by the Red Army, in the Civil War. Armored cars could provide a rallying point for further action or hold back an enemy advance during a retreat. For a brief period of time they could secure a fixed point; and indefinitely, given infantry and artillery support and if properly resupplied.

Armored cars had several operational drawbacks, however. Roads in Russia were sparse and in bad repair. The inevitable bouncing that occurred on irregular roads or terrain naturally contributed to a wide

Austin armored car third production series *Petliura* in the Ukraine, winter 1919. So named for the dedicated Ukrainian nationalist, S.V. Petliura, who had ousted Hetman Skoropadsky's pro-German government and established the Directory early in 1919. The armored car stands on a jack in the rear for repairs. The roundel that appears below the turret and in the rear is in the Ukrainian national colors of light blue (center) and yellow. The name is in yellow or possibly white. Approximately 56 armored cars fell into the hands of the fractious Ukranian forces at the end of 1917. These fought the Reds, Whites, Greens, Blacks and sometimes each other. (Deryabin)

scatter pattern of fire and, consequently, great inaccuracy if firing on the move. Most machine-gun armored cars carried 12–20 belts while most gun vehicles contained 60 artillery rounds. This provision only allowed for perhaps a half-hour of combat before replenishment.

Further, the ranges of armored cars were from a low of 50 to a high of 150 miles (80–250km), the British-produced Austin series coming in at approximately 150 miles. Operational planning and provision for additional fuel could make the difference between an effective combat vehicle and an immobile one, vulnerable to capture. Above all, a simple muddy road or a destroyed bridge could be the dividing line between success or an aborted deployment.

Finally, conditions inside an armored car were not optimal. Temperatures reached 120–140 degrees Fahrenheit (50–60°C); therefore, hatches had to be kept open until actually under fire. Little could be heard by the crew inside due to the chatter of machine guns and roaring of the engine.

Armored cars in the North and Northwest

A few armored cars served with the Whites on the Northern Front, but severe weather, sparse roads and marshy ground confined these to patrols around Archangel. Only one of these, photographed in fall 1919, is known; an Austin third series called *United Russia*.

Two armored cars participated in General Nikolai Nikolaevich Yudenich's offensive on St. Petersburg in October 1919 (known as Petrograd to the Red Army and later Leningrad). The first car, *Russia*, a Fiat, with large, white equal-sided crosses on the front and sides, had captured the second car from the Reds in July. These were attached to the 5th Livenski Rifle Division, 1st Rifle Corps. According to White artillery officer A.S. Gershelman, the cars performed excellently on the relatively good road system near St. Petersburg.

The White Western Army, commanded by Colonel Prince Bermondt-Avalov, owned 10 armored cars of various Russian and German makes. The Western Army, being heavily supplied by Germany, became involved in the geopolitical struggle for the Baltic states rather than supporting Yudenich. The Western Army cooperated with the German Iron Division and the Freikorps, units that possessed at least two more armored cars and two armored trains.

The Estonian Republic emerged as a new state in November 1918, after the collapse of the Russian Empire. By July 1919 the Estonians possessed two armored cars, *Toonela* and *Estonia*. Three more, including a Garford, were captured from the Reds during the Yudenich offensive that fall. In December, after the collapse of the White Northwestern Army, the Estonians merged their five armored cars into their divizion of armored trains.

Armored cars of the Armed Forces of South Russia

Generals L.G. Kornilov, M.V. Alekseev and A.I. Denikin formed the Volunteer Army, a small band of elite volunteers, at Rostov-on-Don in the winter of 1917–1918. Forced into the Kuban by large

Mark V composite tank No. 9085 with British crew at Archangel, North Russian Tank Detachment, late summer 1919. Note white-red-white stripes on the front side. The sponson has been retracted either for ease of movement through the streets or simply to appear less threatening to the local populace. (Tank Museum)

numbers of Red Guards, the volunteers embarked on one of the most remarkable and heroic chapters of military history. These Whites owned no armor during their desperate encounters with Red Guards in the First Kuban Campaign or Ice March. However, Colonel M.G. Drozdovsky's volunteers arrived as reinforcements in May with the armored car *Verni* (Peerless truck chassis, one gun, three machine guns, eight crew).

The Volunteer Army deployed one armored car divizion (a divizion being two or more detachments of armored cars) with six vehicles during the second Kuban campaign in the summer and fall of 1918: *Verni*, *Kornilovets*, *Partizan*, *Kubanets*, *General Markov* and *Dobrovelets*, most having been captured from the Reds. During the campaign, the Kornilov Shock Regiment captured an armored car, renamed the *Kornilovets*, and the *Vityaz* ("Knight") joined the Volunteers. During hard fighting, the crew of the *Vityaz* blew themselves up with their vehicle rather than be captured. In honor of this deed, the Volunteers named a new car *Pamyat Vityaz* (meaning "In Memory of the Knight").

The Armored Car Divizion absorbed more casualties, but continued to grow. The *General Markov* inflicted large losses on the enemy in July at Krylovskaia before being destroyed by artillery in August. That fall the railway workshops at Tikhoretskaia produced three cars, the *General Alekseev*, *Russia* and *Diktator*, built on Burford, Jeffries and White truck chassis. Additional armored cars captured from the Reds at Vladikavkaz in January 1919 brought the total number to 16.

These went through a series of reorganizations as a response to the formation of the Armed Forces of South Russia (AFSR) in February 1919 and ongoing military operations. After shattering the southern front of the Red Army in the spring, Denikin ordered the advance on Moscow. The Volunteer Army moved along the rails, taking Kharkov, Kursk and finally Orel while the Caucasian Army seized Tsaritsyn (later Stalingrad) and the Don Army moved to Voronezh. The left flank of the Volunteers secured Kiev and moved north.

White Russian band entertains Americans at Archangel, 1918–19. The Austin third series armored car is the *United Russia* (white letters). (National Archives)

These extraordinary advances took a heavy toll on the armored cars and many were under repair by the fall. On the other hand, the AFSR acquired new vehicles and had formed additional armored car divizions by September–October 1919 (*see also* Don Cossack armored cars section below):

Volunteer Army (General Mai-Maevsky)
Assigned to Headquarters: *Artillerist*
1st Armored Car Divizion
    Kornilovets, one Fiat, one Düsseldorf, *Lichoi* (all under repair, waiting assignment)
    1st Armored Car Detachment (with elite 1st Corps): *Dobrovolets* (under repair), *General Drozdovsky*, *Kubanets*
    3rd Armored Car Detachment (1st Corps): *Hero* (under repair), *Slavni*, *General Kornilov*
    4th Armored Car Detachment: *General Shkuro* (under repair)
Caucasian Army (General Wrangel)
2nd Armored Car Divizion

All cars undergoing various repairs)

1st Armored Car Detachment: *Nadezhni, Khrabryi, Steregushchi*
2nd Armored Car Detachment: *Vigilant, Brave, Mighty* (all Austin third series)
3rd Armored Car Detachment: *Mstitel, General Markov (II), Doblestnyi Labinets, General Ulagai* (latter two armored tractors)

Independent Forces of Novorossisk Region (region included northern shore of Sea of Azov)
3rd Armored Car Divizion
1st Armored Car Detachment: *Gromoboi, Ilya Mouromets, Krechet*
2nd Armored Car Detachment: *General Slaschev, Orlenok, Redki*
3rd Armored Car Detachment: *Diktator, Krymets* (under repair)

Independent Forces of Kiev Region
2nd Armored Car Detachment: *General Alekseev, Silni, Russia* (gun car)

Reserve Armored Car Divizion
AFSR Headquarters, Taganrog
Also separate detachment operating in North Caucasus, including the *Pamyat Vityaz.*

Each divizion had mobile workshops and tanker and cargo trucks at base headquarters. Whenever possible, cargo trucks, light automobiles and motorcycles accompanied each detachment. A fourth operational divizion began forming at Kiev in October, but probably did not reach full establishment before the general retreat.

The decisive battles in the campaign for Moscow occurred from Orel to Voronezh in October–November 1919. Over-extended and facing a far more numerous and well-supplied enemy, the elite Volunteers fought valiantly for six weeks at Orel. The defeat of the Cossacks at Voronezh and Kastornaia caused the Volunteers to withdraw in good fighting order along the railway to Kursk, Kharkov, Rostov and finally to Novorossisk. Volunteer units in the Ukraine attempted to retreat to the Crimea. The majority of the armored cars had been lost in action or captured by April 1920.

Armored cars of the Russian Army
After the defeat of the AFSR and the evacuation to the Crimea, supreme command devolved on General Baron P.N. Wrangel, who capably set about re-forming the army and restoring morale in April 1920. Wrangel established the Reserve Armored Car and Tank Divizion, which became responsible for training, repair and supply. Two armored car divizions had formed by May at Perekop.

1st Armored Car Divizion
1st Detachment: *Ivan Susanin* (four machine guns, four officers, three soldiers), *Kretchet* (three machine guns, five officers, two soldiers), *Ilya Mouromets* (five machine guns, five officers, one soldier), *Gromoboi* (37mm Hotchkiss gun, 3in. mountain gun, two machine guns, four officers, six soldiers).
3rd Detachment: *Krymets* (three machine guns, four officers, two soldiers), *Diktator* (four machine guns, four officers, two soldiers).

2nd Armored Car Divizion

4th Detachment: *Derzki* (one gun, one machine gun, three officers, two soldiers), *Vityaz* (two machine guns, three officers, two soldiers).

2nd Detachment (being formed).

5th and 6th Detachments (all 6th Detachment cars had 37mm Hotchkiss guns) were eventually established and other armored cars joined the formations: for example, the *Mstitel, Albion, Ekaterinoslavets* and *Gundorovets*. In total, 24 armored cars supported the breakout from the Crimea into the Tauride in June. These participated in all subsequent major operations in the southern Ukraine, including the crossing of the Dnieper and the final retreat back into the Crimea in October.

A colorful example of White ingenuity took place on 2 November against the pursuing regiments of S.M. Budenny's *Konarmiya* (Horse Army). Budenny's orders were to cut the Russian National Army in half, thereby preventing its rallying on the defenses at Perekop. Accompanied by several squadrons of cavalry, 20 White vehicles suddenly appeared in the ranks of the Red cavalry, attacking them in line formation. According to the testimony of one White officer, S. Mamontov, these gray-painted vehicles were improvised mobile fire platforms consisting of three-quarter ton American Ford light trucks, hastily constructed flatbed timber defenses and three machine guns each. These tore a swathe through the enemy ranks, butchering the Reds until evening when the trucks ran out of fuel. No doubt they had played a singular and heroic role in staving off disaster.

In the final days, however, several White armored cars were put out of action, destroyed by their owners or captured. The remaining 17 cars were handed over to the victorious Reds near Kerch by surviving members of the armored car divizions.

Armored cars of the Don Cossacks

Don armored car units began forming on paper in May 1918 under Ataman P.N. Krasnov. Two vehicles were captured from the Reds and repaired at the Don capital in Novocherkassk in August, not an easy task since, according to army commander S.V. Denisov, all necessary parts and skilled workers were absent. The Don Armored Car Divizion possessed six operational vehicles in April 1919, after Ataman A. Bogaevsky assumed leadership of the Don Host.

The **Don Armored Car Division** had emerged by September:

1st Armored Car Detachment: *Ust-Medveditsa* (altered Austin first series, two machine guns, seven crew), *Ataman Kaledin, Steregushchi*.

2nd Armored Car Detachment: *Sokol* (Fiat, two machine guns), *Pecheneg* (Fiat, two machine guns), *Colonel Bezmolitvenni* (one gun, six machine guns, 14 crew)

Mark V composite tank No. 9261 having returned from operations against Petrograd, Estonia, late October 1919. White General Yudenich named the tank *First Aid* in August and the name appears in Russian in white letters on the side in front of the male sponson. The Russian national colors of red, blue and white appear vertically on the front side. The tank rests on a bed of logs, shaved flat on both sides to prevent slippage during transit. Due to the vast distances covered by many military operations and the limited effective range of the tanks, they were normally transported by rail. (Tank Museum)

3rd Armored Car Detachment: *Lugano-Mityakinets* (Austin, two machine guns), *Ust-Belokalitvinets*, *Partizan* (Austin, two machine guns, eight crew, lost shortly thereafter at Berdiansk).

Additional cars: *Kazakh* (Austin, two machine guns, eight crew), *Spolokh* (Lanchester, one gun, one machine gun, eight crew), *Ust-Belokalityinets* (Austin, two machine guns, seven crew), one armored tractor.

Two more were captured from the Reds in October, the *General Kelchevsky* (Austin, two machine guns) and the *General Sidorin* (Garford, 76.2mm mountain gun, two machine guns). A third, the *Ataman Bogaevsky* (Austin third series), may have been a gift from Denikin or the British.

All participated in the advance on Moscow. The *Ataman Bogaevsky* and *General Kelchevsky*, attached to General A.G. Shkuro's 3rd Horse Corps, frequently penetrated Red lines and scattered the cavalry of Budenny's *Konarmiya*. All Don armored cars were lost during the long retreat to Novorossisk.

Armored cars in Siberia and the Far East

Cossack Ataman G.M. Semenov opened the White struggle against the Bolsheviks in Manchuria in the winter of 1917–18. Semenov threw a collection of Cossacks, freebooters and Austrian prisoners of war into an armored car detachment. The largely home-made vehicles consisted of several Italian light truck chassis with Minerva engines. Semenov's brutal lieutenant, Kalmykov, had at least one armored car in his Independent Mixed Ussuri Ataman Kalmykov Division.

Other Cossacks rebelled against Red control. While the Orenburg Cossacks do not seem to have had any armored cars, the Ural Cossacks had several, including the *Zmei Gorynych*, destroyed by the Reds in June 1918. General Denikin reinforced them with several British-produced armored cars early in 1919.

The Civil War along the Volga began in the summer of 1918 when the People's Army or KOMUCH formed a new provisional government in order to oppose the Bolsheviks. Two groups of armored cars participated in the several battles and may have assisted in the capture and defense of Kazan with Colonel V.O. Kappel's elite officer companies and the Czechs. The first unit, the 1st Simbirsk Armored Platoon, consisted of four armored cars and 40 crew. This platoon may have been included in the 1st Kazan Armored Divizion that formed on 27 August.

Admiral A.V. Kolchak assumed power as Supreme Ruler of all the Russias in Siberia in November 1918. An armored car division entered the White order of battle in December, assigned to the Stavka (General Staff) headquartered in Omsk. Three armored cars served in the Ufa Group of General Khanzin's Western Army during the climactic battles for the Volga region in summer 1919. Another of Kolchak's generals, S.N. Rozanov, had one detachment of armored cars in Vladivostok that he used to smash a socialist revolt in the city in November 1919.

Several armored cars were attached to the Czech Legion from 1918–20. Three captured at Penza in May 1918 included the *Grozny* (Garford) and the *Adski* (modified Austin first series). Subsequently, both vehicles served as gun platforms aboard armored trains before ending their careers in the Far East in 1920, once again as armored cars.

Several more were taken from the Red Army during the Czech Legion's anabasis across Siberia in 1918, including a No. 36 Fiat, an Armstrong-Whitworth Fiat, a Fiat-Izhorski, and the *Venomous* (type unknown). Other prizes fell to Czech units dispersed across thousands of miles: one at Kazan, three at Troitsk and an unusual, home-made three-wheeled vehicle in Omsk mounted on a Benz chassis that in turn had been mounted on an armored train.

The Czechs defended Ekaterinburg with several armored cars in September 1918 during the period in which they were instrumental in holding the Ural Front. After Kolchak's assumption of power in November, however, the Legion gradually began to withdraw from the front lines. Throughout 1919 Czech detachments protected a 20-mile strip along the Trans-Siberian Railway from marauding Red and Green partisans. Several armored cars were transferred by the Legion to Kolchak's troops in the course of the year. One White report mentioned a Czech armored car detachment in September 1919 consisting of four vehicles, several motorcycles and one armored train.

WHITE AND ALLIED TANKS IN RUSSIA

The Russians became interested in acquiring tanks after the British successfully employed them on the Western Front in 1916. Shortly before the October Revolution, the Russian Technical Commission in London partly prepaid an order for British tanks, after having noted their essential superiority over the lighter French models. None arrived before the descent into civil war.

Four models of tanks (three British, one French) participated in the Russian Civil War: the heavy Mark V, the Medium Mark A, the Medium Mark B and the French light Renault FT-17.

The first Mark V had arrived in France in January 1918. This heavy tank came with a maximum plate armor of ½in., a crew of eight, stood 8ft 8in. (2.64m) high, with a length of 26ft 5in. (8.06m) and a width of 12ft 9in. (3.89m). Weighing 29 tons, it was only capable of 4.6mph (7.4km/hr). The Russians nicknamed the tank "Ricardo" after the maker of its 150hp engine. Most of the Mark Vs sent to Russia were composites; they carried one "male" sponson with a 6-pdr. gun on one side and a "female" sponson with two Hotchkiss machine guns on the other. Additional machine guns could be carried, one in front, one in the rear and one in the male sponson. In addition to the standard Hotchkiss machine gun, Whites on the Southern Front were known to mount the Russian Maxim, the British Vickers and even the British Lewis machine guns inside the Mark V. The tank could operate for 45 miles (72km) before refueling. This photo shows a Mark V composite tank No. 9417 of the South Russian Tank Detachment, Novorossisk, 1919. The logs, rail ties, skid and blocks have been configured to prevent undue transit movement and to distribute the enormous weight of the tank along the wagon to prevent sagging. These wagons also had to have reinforced springs. The best of these platforms had to be imported from the US. (Tank Museum)

British Royal Tank Corps personnel inspecting Whippet No. A356 at the Baltic Works, Taganrog, southern Russia, summer 1919. The British tank school had originally been established in Ekaterinodar in the Kuban in April, but had moved to Taganrog by June. Some 200 Russian officers had been trained, interchangeably, as drivers and gunners by the end of the year. (Deryabin)

The Whites had no internal factories capable of producing tanks; all had to be imported from Britain and France. Nearly all tanks in the White inventories were British.

Whenever tanks appeared they dominated the battlefield, seizing strongpoints and over-running panicked enemy forces. Only a concentration of Red artillery or Garford gun cars could drive them away. Conversely, the arrival of tanks had an almost magical effect on the Whites. White generals on all fronts consistently requested these from the Allies above all other logistical considerations. British Royal Tank Corps personnel witnessed mounted Kuban Cossacks kissing the sides of tanks in gratitude.

Tanks did have inherent limitations. Due to their limited ranges by road, and far less across country, they had to be transported by train to a point within a few miles of the intended action. Since most Civil War battles took place within 20 miles of a railway, this in itself was not a major limitation. Far more limiting was their vulnerability to mechanical breakdowns. Repairs in the field, perhaps under fire, were understandably difficult. In addition, operational distances had to be considered against the proximity of fuel supplies. A knocked-out bridge, or indeed a bridge too weak to support a tank's weight, could effectively terminate their advance.

The limitations tanks imposed on crews were also considerable. Nicholas Wreden, a junior officer in the White Northwestern Army, described his condition after a full day's combat spent inside the tank *Captain Cromie* in 1919: "every member of the crew was half-poisoned by the odors exuding from the motor, and by the fumes of gunpowder which had accumulated in the tank. The heat inside was terrific, and the steel near the motor scorched one's fingers." Stumbling outside, he pressed his face to the cool, damp ground and vomited.

The primary problem with the tanks, however, was simply that there were not enough of them. Even more importantly, there were never enough fully trained crew, especially on the southern front where the greatest employment of tanks took place.

French tanks in South Russia

The first tanks in Russia arrived at the port of Odessa on the Black Sea on 18 December 1918 in order to reinforce French and Greek divisions facing the Bolsheviks in the southern Ukraine. These tanks, numbering approximately 20, were assigned to the 303rd Company, 1st Battalion, 501st Special Artillery Regiment. These tanks were the Renault FT-17 model. Six "Renos" were lost to the Reds in engagements in February and March 1919. At least six more were left behind for the local Whites during the hasty French evacuation in April.

Rumors persist in Western sources that the French supplied the AFSR with 100 Renaults. These do not appear in White orders of battle and are not mentioned in memoirs. British tank pioneer General J.F.C. Fuller, who inspected Denikin's tanks in August 1919, testified that the Reds had captured six Renault tanks from the French and that three of these had been captured by the Whites.

American tanks in the Russian Far East

Admiral Kolchak urgently requested tanks from the United States in September 1919, just before his spectacular, if short-lived, Tobol offensive. In response, ten American Renault FT-17 tanks arrived in Vladivostok in March 1920; unfortunately, Kolchak was executed by the Reds in February. Bolshevik railway workers learned of the scheme and diverted this shipment to the Amur Red Partisans.

Front of the Mark V composite tank *For Greater Russia*, 1st Tank Detachment, attached to General Baron Wrangel's Caucasian Army, Armed Forces of South Russia, at Tsaritsyn, 1919. Two of the White soldiers wear peasant's hats popular in the Volga region between Astrakhan and Saratov. Note the tarpaulin cover on top. (Deryabin)

Tanks in North Russia

Four British Mark V heavy tanks and two Medium Bs of the North Russian Tank Detachment, commanded by Major J.N.L. Bryan, arrived in the White Sea port of Archangel on 11 August 1919. Officially, the tanks were dispatched to cover the Allied evacuation from Russia. Unofficially, however, they were probably sent in order to test the new Medium B, which had not had such a field opportunity in France.

Three tanks saw brief action along the Vologda Railway in support of an armored train on 29 August, but opportunities to employ the tanks effectively were limited by the immense forests and marshes of North Russia. Headquartered at Solombala on the outskirts of Archangel, the detachment trained Russian volunteers in the use of tanks until final evacuation on 27 September. Ten officers and 24 enlisted men comprised the new North Russian Tank Corps, commanded by Colonel Kenotkenich.

The British left the Corps two tanks, a Mark V (No. 9085) and a Medium B (No. 1613). According to a telegram sent by Kenotkenich to Bryan, these tanks were put to good use in October: "Proud keep traditions, English Tank Corps. Took in glorious fight five fortified points and Plesetskaia Station."

The next months, however, took their toll on the northern Whites as the Red Army, increasingly freed from commitments on other fronts, reinforced the northern sector. As the Whites prepared for evacuation on 19 February 1920, General S.T. Dobrovolsky witnessed the last of the Corps demolishing tank controls and removing the machine guns. Hours before the Bolsheviks entered the city, the tanks were loaded onto barges and sunk in the North Dvina. Enterprising Red engineers subsequently raised these and shipped them to Moscow for analysis.

Tanks in Northwest Russia

The British Northwest Russian Tank Detachment began arriving at Reval, Estonia, on 6 August 1919 to support General N.N. Yudenich's Northwestern Army. Commanded by Lieutenant-Colonel E. Hope-Carson, the detachment comprised 22 officers, 26 enlisted men and eventually six tanks.

The detachment moved east to Narva at the end of August, and Russian personnel began assembling for instruction, 22 officers (of whom ten were

naval), and nine enlisted men. Mixed Anglo-Russian teams were formed into a Tank Battalion. According to Hope-Carson: "The tanks issued to us were Mark V Composite, carrying one 6-pdr. and the usual number of machine guns" (probably five). The names of five of these tanks are known: *First Aid*, *Captain Cromie*, *Brown Bear*, *Liberator* and *White Soldier*.

A Tank Shock Battalion also began forming in early September in order to provide direct infantry support. Led by Captain P.O. Shishko, former commander of the Naval Battalion of Death, the unit numbered 250–400 volunteers.

The Medium A (also called the Whippet) had been conceived in 1917. This medium tank possessed a maximum armor protection of ½in., a crew of four, stood 9ft (2.75m) high with a length of 20ft (6.1m) and a width of 8ft 7in. (2.62m). Weighing 14 tons, the Whippet could achieve a maximum speed of 8.3mph (13.4km/hr) with its twin 45hp Tylor engines; almost twice that of the Mark V, and a rate which allowed it to keep pace with the cavalry. The Medium A carried four Hotchkiss machine guns and had an 80-mile (130km) range. This photo shows three Whippets comprising the 4th Tank Detachment, attached to General Baron Wrangel's Caucasian Army, Armed Forces of South Russia, summer 1919. By October, the detachment had been dispatched to General Denikin's headquarters at Taganrog on the Sea of Azov. By November, the 4th had been attached to the cavalry of the Volunteer Army. Note the open rear doors for ventilation. (Deryabin)

The tanks first had to stabilize a threatening situation at the front before securing Yamburg, on the Russian–Estonian frontier, the natural base for an offensive against Petrograd. The first action took place in early September 1919 southeast of Gdov. Here, Naval Warrant Officer A.S. Strakhov, aboard the *White Soldier*, witnessed the enemy running from their defenses upon seeing the tanks. Subsequently, during 11–15 September, *First Aid*, *Captain Cromie*, *Brown Bear* and the Shock Battalion helped halt a Red breakthrough south of Gdov. Two of the tanks then scattered the Reds at Strugi Belyi on the 28th.

Brown Bear, *First Aid* and *Captain Cromie* assisted in taking the critical point of Yamburg on the Luga River on 11 October. After a gallant rush across the temporary wooden bridge by the Tank Shock Battalion, the Whites occupied the city. The tanks themselves had to cross a shallow ford in the Luga. All tanks had concentrated at Yamburg and had been entrained by 17 October. Meanwhile, White units had pushed to the east and taken Gatchina.

The Allied plan to attack Petrograd involved the Estonians anchoring the left and right flanks of the Whites who would provide the central thrust toward the city. Elements of the British Royal Navy would help the Estonian left neutralize the series of Baltic shore fortifications and keep the Red Navy bottled up at Kronstadt. Unfortunately, according to White veteran V.K. Kuzminim-Karavaev, many of the tanks were worn-out mechanically, and this is evidenced in British records as well. Hope-Carson kept his tanks in two groups of three, the best three on a given day being sent forward while the second group received supplies or repairs.

The tanks reinforced the Whites at Gatchina on 18 October and engaged in a series of firefights over the next week. From Gatchina, effectively a suburb of Petrograd, the Whites planned to advance up the highway to secure Tsarskoe Selo before taking the heights at Pulkovo, which overlooked the prize city itself.

First Aid, Captain Cromie and *Brown Bear* led the initial advance from Gatchina. Red resistance stiffened and several units had to be literally overrun with the tanks. Red artillery, armored trains and hand-picked communist regiments impeded the exhausted and depleted White troops. The Estonians, never resolute in their desire to go beyond their own borders, failed to protect the flanks.

Under pressure from the Allies, Finland had agreed to loan three Renault FT-17 tanks to the Whites and these arrived in time for the fighting around Gatchina on 24–25 October. The Renos formed a separate platoon with Russian crews, one driver and one machine gunner per tank. These returned to Finland later that fall.

By 25 October, all tanks had seen action around Tsarskoe Selo, but were in need of repairs. Commander Bystrumov with a White crew inside *First Aid* struggled toward Pulkovo, which only a few Whites managed to reach. Now outnumbered five-to-one, the Northwestern Army had no choice but to retire.

All Mark Vs were entrained on 26 October for the retreat from Gatchina to Narva. The British transferred the tanks to the Estonians on the condition they continue to oppose Bolshevism and Captain Shishko assumed command of a new tank school near Reval, dedicated to training the Estonians in their use. The Russian tankers disbanded in February 1920.

Tanks in Denikin's Armed Forces of South Russia

12 tanks (six Mark Vs, six Whippets), three officers and 26 enlisted men of the South Russia Tank Detachment arrived in Novorossisk on 22 March 1919. The detachment formed a Tank School at the Kuban capital of Ekaterinodar in April, attached to the British Military Mission under Major-General H.C. Holman. By June, following the front ever-northwards, the Tank School had relocated to the headquarters of the AFSR at Taganrog. Colonel Khaletsky, a former armored car commander who had been a member of the Russian technical delegation to London in 1916, headed the new Russian Tank Corps.

The British Royal Tank Corps trained over 200 Russian volunteer officers with experience in technical arms throughout 1919. The five-week training course emphasized interoperability; that is, each crew member being able to replace another under variable field conditions.

British tank theorist and proponent, General J.F.C. Fuller, visited the combined Tank School and Baltic (repair and assembly) Works in Taganrog in August and September. Fuller met AFSR commander General A.I. Denikin, and both expressed satisfaction at the enthusiasm of the Russian officers doing maintenance while noting their extreme desire to get to the front. Several qualified Russian instructors had been certified to

Mark V composite tank, No. 9186 *Audacious* being inspected by General Sidorin, commander of the Don Cossacks, south Russia, summer 1919. *Audacious* survived the great advance north and the subsequent retreat, both events under General Denikin, commander of the Armed Forces of South Russia. As part of the 1st Tank Detachment, 1st Tank Divizion under General Baron Wrangel in June 1920, *Audacious* participated in breaking the Red lines at Perekop in the Crimea before receiving heavy battle damage. Repaired by the end of the month, *Audacious* moved to Melitopol where the majority of the division's tanks concentrated. The 1st Tank Division next concentrated against the Red bridgehead at Kakhovka on the Dnieper River in October. After breaching the White Crimean defenses, the advancing Red Army captured No. 9186 along with seven other tanks at Sevastopol on 20 November 1920. However, the retreating Whites had hastily destroyed what they could, *Audacious* and others having been "holed" and burned. This photo depicts No. 9186 with the Russian national identification stripes of red, blue and white placed horizontally to the front side of the tank chassis. An elite Kornilov officer stands in the center, top row (see Osprey Men-at-Arms 305: *The Russian Civil War (2) White Armies*). (Deryabin)

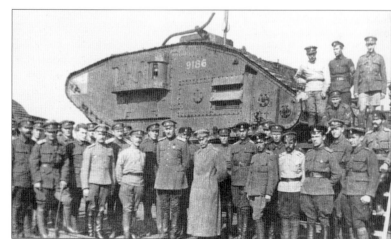

Volunteer Army Medium A Whippet *General Shkuro*, No. A346, moving through Rostov-on-Don, winter 1919–20. Attached to the 4th Tank Detachment, 1st Tank Divizion, No. A346 received its name from the commander of the famous "White Wolves" cavalry (see Osprey Men-at-Arms 305: *The Russian Civil War (2) White Armies*). *General Shkuro* survived the retreat and emerged in June 1920 under General Baron Wrangel, with its same detachment and divizion number, for the attack on Perekop. The tank was subsequently deployed with the 1st Tank Divizion at Melitopol, but details of its end are currently not known beyond the fact it had to be abandoned during the White evacuation from the Crimea in November 1920. British identification stripes of white-red-white are visible on the front of the tank and the word *Shkuro* is in white lettering. (Deryabin)

assist the British in training. Fuller finished his tour by inspecting the tank detachments at Tsaritsyn and Kiev and noted that all 12 original tanks were still in the battle line.

The 1st Tank Divizion (a divizion being two or more tank detachments), had been operational since 15 May and contained four detachments. Theoretically, each detachment was supposed to have up to four tanks, a tractor (American Holt or British Clayton) for pulling a disabled tank from the field, a mobile workshop (British Thornycroft), a half-ton petrol tanker (American Holt), four supply trucks, three automobiles and several motorcycles. These specifications were hard to maintain during the press of civil war.

Each detachment theoretically moved in a train echelon of approximately 15–19 wagons. A flat wagon usually traveled at the front and rear of each train as a precaution against mines, damage to the rails or other ingenious forms of sabotage. A second flat wagon carried spare rails, cross ties and sandbags, then came the locomotive and tender. Additional carriages included up to four reinforced-spring flat wagons for the tanks, up to four flat wagons for the trucks and automobiles, two coaches for passengers, an officers' dining wagon, two for supplies and munitions and one for fuel (gasoline) and lubricants. After arriving at a point for offensive or defensive operations, the tanks would drive down specially prepared ramps that had been affixed to their flat wagons, then remount similarly.

White records show 73 tanks coming in through Novorossisk in 1919, while British indents indicate 74. After the initial distribution of 12 in March, White records note that 16 followed in June, ten in September and a final 35 in early October. Thus, just under half of the tanks arrived when the Whites were at their maximum extension in the campaign for Moscow and when they were so desperately engaged at the front.

A majority of these tanks shipped in October may never have been fully prepared for duties at the front. As evidence for this theory, White orders of battle list 11 tanks still at Novorossisk on 18 November (five of these may have been deployed for defense of the city against active Green partisans), while 11 were still at the Tank School in Taganrog and a further 16 were undergoing repairs (or assembly) at the same location. The White order of battle for mid-October, in fact, listed nine Mark Vs and three Whippets with Wrangel's Caucasian Army, eight Mark Vs and one Whippet with Mai-Maevsky's Volunteer Army, four Whippets with the Don Cossacks, nine Mark Vs and two Whippets at the Tank School, and two Mark Vs at the Baltic Works, for a total of 38.

The White order of battle for 18 November 1919 records 71 tanks in position or in process of formation, the largest grouping of tanks in the Civil War.

1st Tank Divizion

1st Tank Detachment, Volunteer Army: Three Mark Vs (being repaired, Taganrog)

2nd Tank Detachment, Volunteer Army: Three Mark Vs

3rd Tank Detachment, Volunteer Army, Kiev region: Four tanks (Mark Vs and Whippets)

4th Tank Detachment, Volunteer Army, Horse Group: Four Whippets

2nd Tank Divizion

5th Tank Detachment, Volunteer Army: Three Whippets

6th Tank Detachment, Caucasian Army: Four Mark Vs

7th Tank Detachment, Don Army: Four Whippets

8th Tank Detachment, Volunteer Army: Four, probably Mark Vs

Tanks not yet in divizional structure

9th and 11th Tank Detachments: under formation from Tank School and factory

10th Tank Detachment: Four tanks being sent toward Tsaritsyn

Tank School, Taganrog: 11 tanks

At Novorossisk: 11 tanks

At new Nef-Vilde factory, Taganrog, for repairs or final assembly: 16 tanks.

Total: 71

The difference in the number of tanks between the White calculation of 71 and the British tally of 74 may be explained by combat losses, or by mistakes in accounting. The three Renos mentioned by Fuller seem not to have been included in these numbers and may have formed a reserve in the rear for lack of reliable parts.

The first tranche of tanks assisted the Volunteer Army in the beleaguered Don Basin sector throughout May 1919. According to Captain A. Zekhov, their arrival put the majority of Reds to flight. Defectors intimated that their commissars had told them the tanks were merely mobile cardboard props and not to be feared.

During May, one Mark V boldly engaged a Red armored train, putting it out of action until a second Red train arrived and hit the tank five times throughout the hull. According to later evidence, this Mark V seems to have been salvaged and refitted for the front by September. Similarly, in April 1920 in the Crimea, the Whites would attack the Red armored train *Coal Miner* with three tanks, causing it to withdraw after receiving damage. Nevertheless, in 1919, AFSR headquarters, placing exceptional value on tanks, expressly forbade tank versus armored train duels.

The light Renault FT-17 had become operational in France in early 1918. This two-man tank had a driver up front, a gunner in the turret, and could be configured with one 8mm Hotchkiss machine gun or one 37mm gun. The armor varied between ¼ to ½in. (over ¾ of an inch on the sides of the gun-model turret). The Russians nicknamed this tank "Reno" after the maker's name. Although weighing only 6 tons, the tank's 35hp engine could manage no more than 4.8mph (7.5km/hr) and 22 miles (35km) range by road. The Reno had a height of 7ft (2.13m), length of 16ft 5in. (5.02m) (including tail) and a width of 5ft 9in. (1.74m). This photo details the retreat of the Armed Forces of South Russia, February–March 1920. From left to right standing on immobile rail wagons, a Mark V, two Renault FT-17s and a Medium A. Probable location is along the Rostov–Bataisk–Novorossisk rail line. (Tank Museum)

The single most dramatic tank action in 1919 occurred in June at Tsaritsyn (later Stalingrad), a highly fortified city on the Volga which the Don Cossacks had tried to take throughout 1918. Proudly referred to in Bolshevik sources as the "Red Verdun," Tsaritsyn was the supply and communications artery between the southeastern front and Red divisions operating in the Trans-Caspian regions. Seizure by the Whites additionally offered the prospect of making contact with Kolchak's left flank west of the Urals.

According to White veteran A. Trembovelsky, all 1st Divizion tanks (16) were deployed with Wrangel's Caucasian Army against Tsaritsyn during the second half of June. However, many of these did not see consistent action because of lack of fuel. The main attack occurred on 29 June, with the tanks of 1st Detachment (three Mark Vs) and 4th Detachment (3 Whippets) leading. Two of the tanks broke down during transit, but the other four smashed through the rolls of barbed wire and turned to drag them apart, forcing holes in the wire defenses. White supporting units followed as the tanks moved parallel to the trench lines and cleared away the defenders.

The Kuban Cossacks entered Tsaritsyn in force the next day and garnered 40,000 prisoners, 10,000 train wagons, 151 locomotives, 70 guns, 300 machine guns and the armored trains *Lenin* and *Trotsky*. Denikin visited the city and on 3 July ordered all units of the Armed Forces of South Russia to advance and take Moscow before Christmas. Meanwhile, the tanks of 1st Divizion transferred to Taganrog to repair and refit.

Few records have survived about tank operations in the fall of 1919. Detachments defended Tsaritsyn and moved west to Kiev and advanced from Kharkov to Kursk and then Orel, the farthest point north attained by the AFSR. Due to the rapid White advances and the need for the tanks to travel long distances by train, there were few opportunities to concentrate them against a fixed position at the level of divizion.

One example testifies to the ability of the tanks, especially the Whippet, to work with cavalry. At the end of September, General Ulagai's 2nd Kuban Corps and the 4th Tank Detachment routed the 1st Don Red

A handful of tanks survived the disastrous evacuation of the port of Novorossisk in April 1920. The harbor had only one floating crane available, called the *Feodosia*, for maneuvering the heavy tanks from quay to ship. Note the Mark V in the center of the photo being winched aboard ship. (Tank Museum)

Cavalry near Kotluban. The tanks, having been disguised as haystacks, awaited the charge of the Red cavalry before emerging to wreak havoc with their machine guns.

During the winter retreat, tanks were often detrained to hold a station long enough for retreating troops to escape. Indeed, General Holman, renowned for his exploits with Lewis guns and aircraft, personally commandeered one tank for this purpose. Tanks also covered the withdrawal of the British mission from Taganrog and the evacuation from Novorossisk. By April 1920 the Reds had captured 50 British Mark Vs and Whippets. The Russian Tank Corps had temporarily ceased to exist.

Tanks in Wrangel's Russian Army

The **1st Tank Divizion** reformed in Wrangel's Russian Army in the Crimea in May 1920; repair facilites were located at Sevastopol. Given a drastically reduced front, White armored units were able to concentrate more effectively, a fact noted by the Red high command. By 7 June the tanks had been reorganized as follows:

1st Detachment: (Mark Vs) *Grozny, General Slaschev, Loyal, Audacious, Great Russia, Mighty Russia* (renamed *Slaschev* in June after the loss of its sister tank)

2nd Detachment: (Whippets) *Sphinx, Tiger, Stepnya, Crocodile* (renamed *Siberian* in June)

3rd Detachment: (Mark Vs) *For Holy Russia, Field Marshal Kutusov, General Suvorov, General Skobelev, Field Marshal Potemkin, For Faith and Fatherland*

4th Tank Detachment: (Whippets) *Sadko, General Wrangel, General Shkuro, Urals* (transferred to 2nd Detachment on 10 June)

Detached Platoon: (Renault FT-17) *Modest, Gray*

Wrangel planned the breakout from the Crimea into the fertile Tauride for 7 June. Red 13th Army had dug in on the isthmus at Perekop and to the east at Chongar. The moment seemed propitious because the Reds had gone to war with Poland. However, the British informed him that an offensive northward would result in the withdrawal of their military mission; consequently, the British tankers left by the end of the month.

White Army armored train, equipped with naval gun, in North Russia, 1918–19. The top photo shows the unarmored locomotive and artillery wagon. The naval gun has a canvas cover over the muzzle for transportation. The crew has a mixed complement of White soldiers and sailors, judging from other photos in the series. Half of the artillery wagon has been fitted with a protective roof. The wagon is unarmored, being wooden with strip metal reinforcements. The bottom photo depicts the gun ready to fire through a lowered platform in the side, which is also the entry point into the wagon via the ladder. (National Archives)

Wrangel broke the Perekop and Chongar bottlenecks by a classic application of naval, aerial and armored assets. Appreciating that the Reds had earmarked special artillery units to knock out the tanks, the Whites formed their own special group of horse artillery to provide counter-battery fire. The tanks were equipped with special mufflers to mask their advance and with hawsers that could grapple and destroy the wire defenses.

Tanks of the 1st and 4th Detachments plunged into the Red defenders at Perekop and ultimately carried the field. However, an elite Latvian division, supported by artillery, counter-attacked close-in with grenades and disabled three tanks. Meanwhile, 3rd Detachment and the Detached Platoon, encountering lighter resistance, broke the Chongar defenses. The paths into the Tauride had been cleared.

The next months involved establishing positions along the Dnieper River, which formed the White left flank from Kherson to Alexandrovsk (later Zaporozhye), and on the right flank in the open country from Alexandrovsk to the Sea of Azov at Berdiansk. The 1st Tank Division concentrated at Melitopol, roughly the center of the White positions, on the main railway from the Crimea into the Tauride and fought as detachments in consolidating this perimeter. Both sides recognized the strategic value of Kakhovka on the Dnieper because a Red breakthrough there could split the White army in two and jeopardize any retreat back into the Crimea.

Two events ultimately became decisive for the Whites in August. First, the Poles defeated the Reds in the "Miracle of the Vistula" and the warring parties began negotiating an armistice that would free enormous Red reserves for transfer to the southern front. Second, the Reds managed to cross the Dnieper and establish a bridgehead at Kakhovka. The tanks conducted their last divizion-level operation against that bridgehead in October.

Red engineers constructed three defensive zones at Kakhovka, an external line of trenches, a base line of trenches and wire and an inner line of trenches. Anti-tank ditches and minefields covered anticipated approaches and artillery and machine-gun positions had been sited for maximum effect. The Whites understood that, once inside the perimeter, their supporting units would be outnumbered two-to-one; nevertheless, the liquidation of the bridgehead would disrupt the deployment of massive Red reinforcements from the Polish front. During a preliminary clash in September, 2nd Detachment lost the *Sphinx* and *Siberian*.

The main armored battle commenced on 14 October, 12 operational tanks advancing line abreast, just within sight of each other, shrouded in the gloom of the early morning. Mobile artillery first probed the external defenses and then the base line. Infantry, cavalry and the 1st Armored Car Divizion followed to exploit the breakthrough. Breaching the external line, the tanks arrived at the base line and encountered heavy resistance. Red artillery, Garfords and mortars knocked out several tanks and one fell to grenades. White infantry had failed to follow up.

The Reds counter-attacked at noon but were held in check by the Whites until the 16th. In all, nine tanks had been put out of action: the Whites managed to recover four. Only three undamaged tanks remained besides the Renault platoon that had been left in the Crimea for lack of parts. The Whites sabotaged all of these prior to evacuation in November.

WHITE ARMORED TRAINS

Russia possessed 37,000 miles (60,000km) of railway track, the majority being five-foot gauge, at the end of 1917. The Russian Army had used several armored trains in World War I, but these fell to the Reds, Ukrainians and Central Powers during the Bolshevik Revolution. The Whites on all fronts began with nothing.

The Whites had no specific standard configuration for their armored trains. Most trains had to be captured from the Reds and modified, using available armaments and materials, while the remainder had to be built from scratch on flat wagons in the few factories under White control that still retained sufficient industrial capacity. Nevertheless, certain principles were understood.

Locomotives and tenders (tenders carried coal or wood for fuel) were always placed in the center of an armored train formation, known as an echelon, for protection. Moreover, if the front or rear wagons were damaged, the locomotive could disentangle and move surviving elements of the echelon to safety. Locomotives usually had gun and machine-gun cars, one or two of each, immediately to the front and rear.

To the extreme front and rear were flat wagons, either empty or filled with non-critical supplies. Enemy forces in the Civil War packed flat wagons with explosives, similar to the fire ships of old, and drove these down the rails to demolish armored trains. Tracks were also mined or prepared for demolition at the appropriate moment. Thus, the flat wagons would absorb the initial shock. Additional flat wagons in the front and rear contained engineering materials, including lengths of rail and lumber for making minor repairs.

Light armored trains generally had one to four artillery pieces inside revolving turrets on armored wagons or merely mounted on platforms on sandbagged and reinforced flat wagons. These trains could carry standard field pieces or howitzers. Heavy armored trains had one or two guns of heavier caliber, including naval models, usually mounted inside relatively open, reinforced-spring flat wagons. Each configuration could carry anything from four to 20 machine guns.

Armored trains sported a wide variety of guns and machine guns. Most weapons were Russian. However, the Allies contributed a substantial number of pieces to the White inventory. The British supplied artillery to Denikin's Whites of the south, to Kolchak's Siberians, to the northern Whites at Archangel and Murmansk, and to a lesser extent to the North-western Army. The French sent military aid to Kolchak, but gave special preference to the Czechs. The White warlords of the Russian Far East often used Japanese arms.

These armaments dated from World War I, which overlapped the Russian Civil War in 1918. Standard Russian arms included the Putilov 76.2mm field gun (Models 1900, 1902, 1913), the 76.2mm mountain gun (Models 1904, 1909), the 6-in. howitzer and the 7.62mm Maxim machine gun.

Since 1892, the Russians had produced heavy naval guns under license from the French designer, Canet: these included 120mm (5.75in.), 152mm (6in.), and 75mm (2.9in.) guns. By 1917, 523 of the 6-in. had been produced along with 799 of the 75mm. Additionally, the Russians had produced the 47mm Hotchkiss gun under French license.

The British supplied the Whites with their 18-pdr and 60-pdr field guns, the naval 12-pdr, the 4.5-inch howitzer and Vickers and Lewis machine guns. French 75mm Puteaux field guns found their way in smaller numbers to the Whites of the north, to the White Siberians and to the Czechs. Japanese arms contributed to the Whites of the Far East included the 75mm Type 38 field gun and the 70mm Battalion Howitzer Type 92.

All these weapons (and more), both Russian and Allied, variously found their way onto White armored trains according to need and availability. Unfortunately for posterity, White orders of battle and memoirs often did not religiously record exact makes or calibers allotted to specific trains, though these details are included in this text where they are known.

Crews of armored trains, which in the White armies tended to be 50–120 strong, often maintained two shifts, one on the train and one living in passenger wagons back at the base in reserve. A few trains carried a mobile platoon or company that could capture and hold a strategic point until the main supporting force caught up. The speeds of these trains were generally in the range 12–30mph (20–48km/hr).

Railways were central to the planning of most military operations during the Civil War period and armored trains were vital for controlling the rails and seizing stations and railheads. Armored trains provided direct and indirect offensive and defensive fire and could easily be switched from one sector to another. Control of a line enabled friendly tanks, armored cars and troop trains to move up in echelon and debouch at the front while, conversely, denying this ability to the enemy. If a sector were lightly garrisoned by defensive artillery, armored trains could force the position and linger in the rear of the enemy, allowing friendly forces to consolidate the field.

Armored trains, however, did come with a few liabilities. Railways and bridges in their path had to be in reasonable repair. Enemy forces which severed the rails to the rear of the trains at least temporarily stranded them and, in the case of a major offensive, could cause them to be

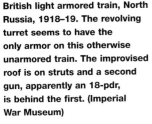

British light armored train, North Russia, 1918–19. The revolving turret seems to have the only armor on this otherwise unarmored train. The improvised roof is on struts and a second gun, apparently an 18-pdr, is behind the first. (Imperial War Museum)

abandoned altogether. Acts of nature such as mud- or rock-slides, and even vagaries in the weather such as snow and ice, could menace the steel roads. Czech Legionnaire Gustav Becvar noted an armored train having to move forwards and backwards repeatedly to break up the ice forming on the rails in the cold November at Ekaterinburg in 1918. Moreover, train armor offered protection only from bullets and shell splinters; direct hits, unless glancing off curvature in the plating, tended to go straight through.

Armored trains in East Russia

Kolchak's White Siberians had at least four armored echelons operating west of the Urals during the offensive for the Volga in May 1919. These may have been distributed equally between General Pepeliev's Siberian Armored Train Divizion and General Gaida's 1st Independent Divizion of Armored Trains. General Rouquerol of the French Military Mission noted the lack of armored trains in Kolchak's inventory.

The White warlord, Ataman Semenov, variously had 14 armored trains operating between Lake Baikal, Manchuria and Vladivostok under the command of General N. Bogomolets. These included: *Semenovets, Ataman, Grozny, Cossack, Zabailkalets, Otvakhny, Master, Horseman, Stanichnik, Valiant, Swift* and *Just.* The Americans identified another, the Destroyer, which they captured at Verkhne-Udinsk after Bogomolets threatened to fire on them. This train had two 3-in. guns, two 1-in., 10 machine guns, ½in. thick armor reinforced by 18in. of concrete, and a crew of 57. Semenov's nominal lieutenant, Ataman Kalmykov, possessed at least one command train in the American sector near Khabarovsk.

The Americans, consistent with the Allies in general, constructed only light armored trains. Company garrisons created mobile dormitories out of box or sleeper wagons wherever local conditions could not support more permanent quarters. Over 300 American engineering personnel formed the Russian Railway Service Corps under the overall Inter-Allied Railway Committee. The Corps maintained the railways until May 1920.

The British contributed three armored trains, two with two 12-pdrs and one with a 6-in. naval gun, compliments of HMS *Suffolk*, which had anchored off Vladivostok in January 1918. These guns were mounted on flat wagons in August and entered operations along the Ussuri River against marauding Red partisans. At the end of August, the 12-pdrs and 6-in., now in the same echelon, commenced a 6,105-mile (9,800km) journey west to the Volga Front, arriving at Ufa on 12 November.

American light armored train in North Russia near Medvejya Gora, northern shore of Lake Onega, *circa* May 1919. The metal sheeting on the artillery wagon has been hastily hammered out and would stop little beyond bullets. British General Maynard had requested American railway troops for securing his advance south from Murmansk and had received them in April. Maynard wrote: "Every man of their 600 was a volunteer, full of enthusiasm and the love of adventure." (Imperial War Museum)

A1: Don Cossack armored car *Medveditsa*, summer 1919

A2: Volunteer Army armored car *Mighty*, 1919

B1: Renault FT-17 tank, 1920

B2: Medium Mark A Whippet tank *Sphinx*, 1920

C1: Mark V tank No. 9261 *First Aid*, Northwest Russia, 1919

C2: Medium Mark B tank, No. 1613, North Russia, 1919

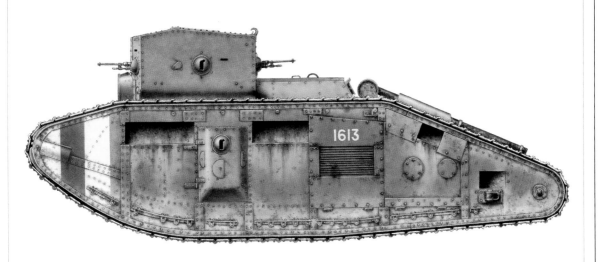

D: MARK V COMPOSITE TANK No. 9358

KEY

1 Track idler wheel
2 Brake pedal
3 Clutch pedal
4 Front machine gunner seat
5 Two driving control handles
6 Front Hotchkiss machine gun mount
7 Peephole cover
8 Front superstructure (cab) upper hatch
9 Officer's locker
10 Driver's window and flap
11 Driver's window flap securing chain
12 Speed change handle
13 Forward-reverse handle
14 Driver's instrument panel
15 Driver's seat
16 Ricardo engine compartment
17 Engine compartment hinged sidewalls
18 Silencer
19 Exhaust pipe
20 Engine air compressor
21 Engine air intake
22 Rear superstructure (cab)
23 Folding wall
24 Vision slit
25 Gun port cover
26 Right (port) side doors under machine-gun sponson
27 Semaphore mast
28 Rear munitions storage
29 Semaphore mast handles
30 Epicyclic gear cover
31 Cooling system water tank
32 Rear upper hatch
34 Fire extinguisher
35 Radiator housing
36 Return roller with track guide rings
37 Rear machine gun ball mount
38 Oil tank
39 Track cleaning plate
40 Fuel tank compartment
41 Track guide rails
42 Track
43 Towing shackle
44 Rear grille
45 Drive sprocket
46 Final drive
47 Roller with track guide rings
48 Sleek roller
49 Driving chain
50 Petrol tanks
51 Fuel cap
52 Louvres
53 Radiator fan
54 Brake drums
55 Gear box
56 Engine hand-starter crank stand
57 Hand-starter crank
58 Magneto
59 Gun sponson door
60 Gun sponson machine gun ball mount
61 Gunner protective shield
62 Pistol grip gun handle and trigger
63 Breech-block
64 Munitions storage under gun mount
65 Gun sight
66 Revolving gun shield
67 Gun sponson
69 Swiveling armored gun cover
70 Munitions storage
71 Revolver case
72 Track tension adjuster

SPECIFICATIONS

Crew: Eight (commander, driver, six gunners)

Combat weight: 29 tons

Power-to-weight ratio: 5.2 horsepower per ton

Length: 26ft 5in.

Height: 8ft 8in.

Width: 12ft 9in.

Width for conveyance by rail: approximately 8ft 9in.

Engine: Ricardo, six-cylinder inline, 150hp at 1,200rpm

Transmission: four forward gears, one reverse

Petrol capacity: 93 Imperial gallons

Petrol consumption: 2 Imperial gallons per mile

Maximum speed: 4.6 miles per hour

Maximum range: 45 miles

Gun: 6-pdr., 23-cal. Q.F. (quick firing) Hotchkiss gun (183-shell and 24-case shot in storage)

Gun traverse: 100 degrees

Gun depression/elevation: –15 to +25 degrees

Machine guns: Five 8mm Hotchkiss machine guns (in boxes of 250–300 rounds for approximately 6,000–6,750 total rounds. According to Major J.N.L. Bryan, commander of the North Russian Tank Detachment, all his tanks had "new" .303-cal. rounds in August 1919.

Armor: 14mm front, 12 to 8mm on superstructure (cabs), 8mm engines and gear, 12mm sponsons, 10mm hull sides, 8mm hull roof and rear, 6mm hull

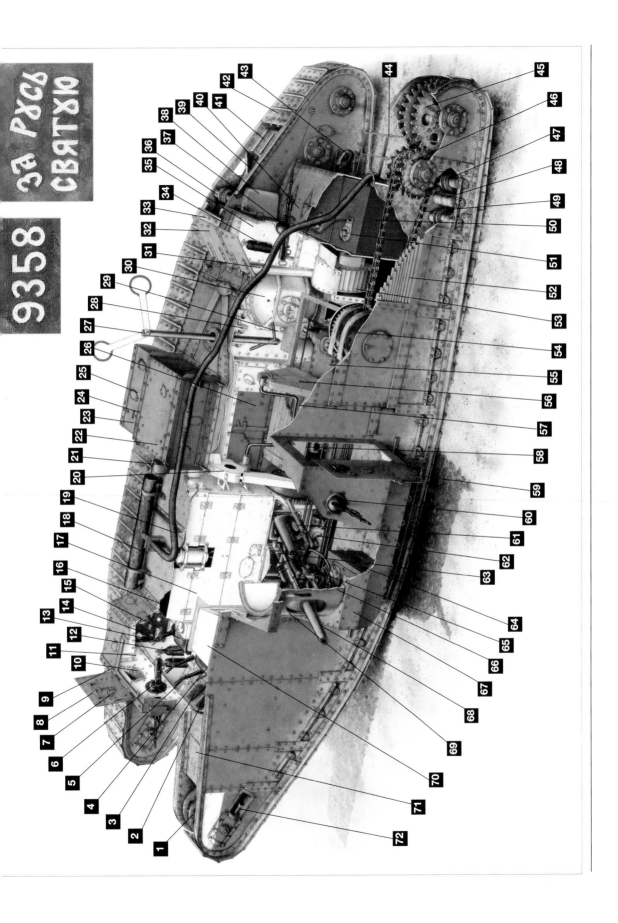

9358

ЗА РУСЬ СВЯТУЮ

E1: Czech armored motor wagon *Zaamurec*, Siberia 1919–20

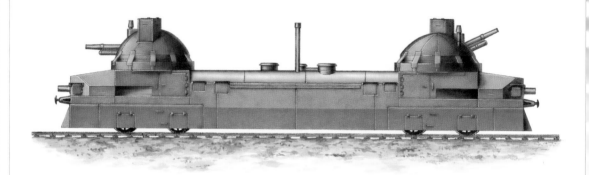

E2: Czech armored train *Orlik*, central Siberia, 1919–20

F1: Volunteer Army, armored train *Forward for Fatherland*, summer 1918

ЗА ВѢРУ, ЦАРЯ И ОТЄЧЕСТВО

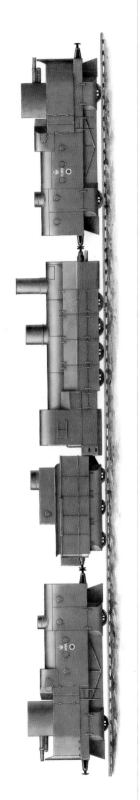

F2: Volunteer Army, armored train *Officer*, February 1919

ОФИЦЕРЪ

**G1: Volunteer Army, armored train *To Moscow*,
winter 1919–spring 1920**

9 48878

9 49922

G2: White Siberian armored train *Vityaz*, fall 1920

The 12-pdrs and the 6-in. then split into separate echelons and created such havoc in December that the local Reds were given orders to "cut the throats" of any British crew captured. In 1919 crew from HMS *Kent* relieved the original crew, carrying with them a 6-in. gun as a replacement for the worn-out earlier piece. From early May to the end of June the guns served aboard the White Navy's Kama Flotilla on the Kama River before being married up again as an armored train echelon during the White retreat from Perm. The crew volunteered to form a Special British Naval Armoured Train while in Omsk, but after the plan's rejection by British authorities, continued their withdrawal to Vladivostok, which they reached in August.

The real masters of the rails in Siberia were the Czechs with their 50,000 legionnaires and 32 armored trains. The Czech Legion coordinated operations with the Allied Military Mission in Siberia until its evacuation in 1920. The Legion took an active role in capturing or defending the Volga cities of Samara, Simbirsk and Kazan and the industrial cities of the Urals including Ekaterinburg and Chelyabinsk.

Moving east, their units cleared the Trans-Siberian Railway of Reds from Omsk to Vladivostok. After heavy fighting on the Urals front in the fall of 1918, the Legion progressively became a defensive force guarding the railway upon which it depended to return home. Each regiment defended a sector of the rail line, including a 10-mile (16km) corridor on either side, each regiment possessing between one and four armored trains. Most of these were lightly armored, with one or more wagons reinforced with sandbags or a few metal plates to provide posts for machine guns, or one or two field guns on concrete mountings.

The 4th Regiment's *Grozny* had a Garford armored car mounted on a flat wagon and 10 machine guns. This regiment also possessed the Legion's most celebrated armored train, the Orlik. The Legion kept a reserve group of six trains as a striking force between the Western Front and the Einesei River: *Ordernik, Tesin, Mariinsk, Tajset, Spasitel* and the 2nd Light Battery.

Armored trains in North Russia

Only two railways existed on the Northern Front: Murmansk to Petrograd and Archangel to Vologda. Offensive operations south from Archangel necessarily involved rail movement because of the dense forest and marsh in the region. The 425-mile (680km) rail section to Vologda passed over 262 wooden bridges, severely impeding any advance. The Reds could merely blow one bridge, retreat out of range, and repeat the process.

The British had two armored trains at Archangel by September 1918 and the French at least one. The future Lord Kennett commanded the *Miles* during the attack on Chiama Bridge on 31 August. This train had two 12-pounders, a howitzer at the fore (probably a British 4.5-in.) and several machine guns (probably Vickers and Lewis).

British officer inspecting American train repair shop in North Russia, 1918–19. (Imperial War Museum)

French light unarmored train with camouflaged 75mm field gun in North Russia, 1918–19. The flag belongs to one of the small French contingents at Archangel. The artillery wagon has only the most rudimentary defense of split logs and sandbags. (Imperial War Museum)

The Whites had two armored trains at Archangel in May 1919, the *Admiral Kolchak* and the *Admiral Nepenin*, both with naval guns and crews. Two more were under construction by August, the *General Denikin* and *Lip.* Red 6th Army intelligence noted two trains at Oberskoi in spring 1919, the first armed with two 6-in. guns and the second with four 3-in. anti-aircraft guns.

British-led Syren Force, operating south from Murmansk had at least two armored trains by May 1919, one White, one American. American railway engineers constructed a light train with steel plates and sandbags and fitted Lewis guns and at least one field piece. The White train came with British ordnance: two 4.5-in. howitzers and an 18-pdr.

The Allies had evacuated north Russia by the fall of 1919, leaving the Whites to fight alone. All trains in the north fell to the advancing Reds by February 1920. The crews of the *Admiral Kolchak* and *Admiral Nepenin* were executed.

Armored trains in the Northwest

The Northwest Front had a good system of rails, especially considering the short distance from the Estonian border to Petrograd: main trunk routes connected Reval, Narva, Pskov and Petrograd. The North-western Army had four armored trains for the offensive on Petrograd in 1919: the *Admiral Essen*, *Admiral Kolchak*, *Pskovite* and *Talabchanin*, the first two with predominately naval crews.

Veteran A.C. Gershelman described the *Admiral Essen*, which had been painted black. From front to rear, the echelon consisted of a front platform with engineering materials, a gun wagon with a 3-in. gun mounted on a wooden semi-circle, a wagon with one or two small naval pieces, a machine-gun wagon, locomotive, another machine-gun wagon, and finally a platform wagon. Among its many encounters, the *Admiral Essen* engaged the Red armored train *Volodarsky* in July 1919 and both received battle damage before retiring.

Artillery wagon *Wambola* of an unknown Estonian armored train, 1919. Many wagons of Estonian armored trains carried individual names, the train itself having a further name. The Estonians have cut away half of a standard boxcar and riveted sheets of steel along the sides. Note entry steps to the right and closable steel window in the center. A tarpaulin above and canvas barrel-cover protect the howitzer. (Deryabin)

Estonian artillery wagon with naval gun, name unknown, still with Tsarist emblem on the side, probably winter, 1918–19. The side of the wagon lowers to allow for traverse. Chains connect the wagon with the rails underneath for stability during firing. (Deryabin)

Veteran Nicholas Wreden served six months of 1919 aboard the *Admiral Kolchak* as an artillery observer before transferring to tanks. When not in the observer's turret directing fire, Wreden and a small party would establish an observation post connected to the train by telephone wire. The crew of 300 also included a naval landing company which could secure bridges or track. On one occasion, the company even captured a battery of three 6-inch guns. Before going into battle, the crew usually received a briefing from headquarters. Action tended to be continuous in 1919, crew members seldom getting more than a day's rest between missions. By campaign's end, the *Admiral Kolchak* had worked with every division in the Northwestern Army, advancing with the infantry wherever possible and providing covering fire during retreats. The train returned to base every week to replenish munitions.

The *Admiral Kolchak* had two field guns and 20 machine guns. Armor consisted of scrap iron around the engine and observation turret. Bags of cement and sand protected the roofed regulation freight wagons which housed the numerous crew. The artillery wagons had large sections of the roofs and walls removed in order to traverse the guns and this inevitably exposed the gunners to hostile fire.

Despite sterling service, the armored trains and their supporting arms failed to cut the rails south of Petrograd in October, a mistake that allowed Red reinforcements to enter the city. All White armored trains managed to fall back on Estonia in November except the *Pskovite*.

Armored trains of Denikin's Volunteer Army
The Volunteer Army captured several armored trains, including three at Tikhoretskaia during the second Kuban campaign in the summer of 1918. Six were in the White inventory by September:

1st Reserve Train (from November light armored train *General Alexiev*; one gun wagon, one machine-gun wagon)

2nd Reserve Train (from November light armored train *General Kornilov*; one 3-in. gun, one 47mm Hotchkiss gun, one machine-gun wagon)

3rd Reserve Train (from November light armored train *Forward for Fatherland*; one 75mm gun wagon, one 3-in. gun wagon, one machine-gun wagon)

4th Reserve Train (from November light armored train *Officer*; one gun, seven machine guns)

5th Reserve Train (from November *Battery of Distant Battle* and later the heavy armored train *United Russia*; two 105mm guns, two 120mm Canet gun, two 47mm Hotchkiss gun, three machine guns)

Additional: *Naval Battery of Distant Battle No. 2* (later light armored train *Dmitry Don*; four 75mm naval guns, one 47mm Hotchkiss gun, five machine guns)

These trains fought continuously in the Kuban that fall and at Stavropol, Armavir, and along the Black Sea Coast. By January 1919 the Whites had captured eight more armored trains in the North Caucasus and seven more were under construction, including the *Knight* (two guns, five machine guns).

The Armed Forces of South Russia formed that January under General Denikin, the original Volunteers being joined by the Don and Kuban Cossacks and the Crimean-Azov Army. The year 1919 on the Southern Front would witness the largest concentrations of armored trains in the history of the Russian Civil War.

Don Cossack armored trains

Ataman Krasnov ordered the establishment of the Don Armored Railway Battery, consisting of three trains, under engineer Lieutenant Colonel N.I. Kondyrin in August 1918. Over the next weeks, this formation expanded into the Don Railway Brigade. One White armored train comprised a "battery," while two or more batteries equaled a "divizion."

1st Divizion

Ataman Kaledin, Gundorovets (each with two guns), *Prince Suvorov* (four guns)

2nd Divizion

Razdorets, Mityakinets (each with two guns), *Ilya Mouromets* (four guns)

3rd Divizion

Partisan Colonel Chernetsov, Kazak Zemlyanukhin, General Baklanov

Czech armored train in Siberia. The locomotive and tender are armored with large plates of steel. (Imperial War Museum)

4th Divizion
Don Bayan, Ermak, Ivan Krug

Detached
Ataman Orlov, Ataman Nazarov

Northern Front
Three trains, including *Buzuluk* and *Khoper*

These trains normally consisted of two armored flat cars with two 3-in. guns and 14 machine guns. Crews theoretically approximated nine officers and 100 enlisted men, half of whom were to be ethnic Don Cossack. Officers were seconded from the Don artillery.

The geography of the Don region had few natural defenses and the Cossacks had to be mobile in order to defend or advance their fluid borders. In addition to actions at Leski, Kupiansk and Zverevo-Shterovka, Krasnov attacked Tsaritsyn three times in the fall and winter of 1918. Don trains engaged their more numerous Red counterparts several times but the Cossacks ended the year unable to take the Red Verdun.

1st Regiment
Ermak, Ataman Orlov, Razdorets, Ivan Krug (renamed *Don Ataman Bogaevsky* in October), *Gundorovets, Azovets* (renamed *General Guselshchikov* in September), *Mityakinets, Ataman Platov*

2nd Regiment
Ilya Mouromets, Colonel Chernetsov, General Baklanov, Kazak Zemlyanukhin, Ataman Kaledin, Ataman Samsonov, Atamanets, General Mamontov

Detached or in brigade
1st and 2nd Naval Heavy Batteries with Canet guns.

The Don Cossacks also possessed a considerable number of heavy guns that were formed into the 1st–9th Batteries of Naval Heavy Artillery early in 1919. Each battery of two guns could be mounted on platform wagons and used as heavy armored trains, or placed on barges as floating batteries as part of the River Forces of South Russia. For example, 4th, 6th and 8th Batteries operated on the Volga while the 5th and 7th were based at Ekaterinoslav in the Dnieper River. All batteries had 152mm Canet naval guns except the 7th (8-inch naval guns) and the 8th (British guns mounted on tractors). Most of the heavy batteries were assigned to the artillery of the AFSR in November and within two months had been transferred to service with the heavy armored trains along the front and renamed.

Armored trains of the AFSR in 1919–20

The number of armored trains in the AFSR expanded rapidly from the early weeks of 1919. Throughout that spring, General Mai-Maevsky conducted the most brilliant railway campaign in history against enemy forces numbering five times his own. Using the intricate railway system in the Don Basin, the elite Volunteers shuttled from sector to sector in troop trains supported by the armored trains, ultimately shattering the 8th and 13th Red Armies.

The *Zaamurec* motor wagon of the Czech armored train *Orlik*, Trans-Siberian Railway. Note the twin revolving turrets and the observer posts on top. (National Army Museum)

The Volunteer Army then moved north, seizing Kharkov in June and Kursk in September, while simultaneously moving west into the Ukraine and taking Ekaterinoslav in June, Poltava in July and Kiev in September. Red resistance in the Crimea ceased by the end of May. Meanwhile, Wrangel had broken the Reds on the Manych line in May and pursued them to Tsaritsyn, capturing the city at the end of June.

Armored trains moved with the main columns along each axis of advance. Infantry in carts traveled the country roads that often followed the rails while the cavalry provided reconnaissance on each side. Echelons carrying troops, armored cars, tanks and command cars followed. When available, White aircraft circled overhead.

By October the AFSR possessed the largest number of armored trains of any White force in the Civil War. The following order of battle (18 October 1919) has been compiled from several sources, including official documents and memoirs:

Volunteer Army
1st Corps
2nd Armored Train Divizion: *General Kornilov, Officer, Ivan Kalita*
4th Armored Train Divizion: *Orel, Glory to the Officer, Grozny*
6th Armored Train Divizion: *General Drozdovsky*
9th Armored Train Divizion: *Victorious Thunder, Drozdovtsi, Soldier, Valor of the Knight*
Kiev Forces
3rd Armored Train Divizion: *Knight, Dmitry Don, Prince Pozharsky* and *Bayan* (detached)
Novorossisk Forces
5th Armored Train Divizion: *General Markov, Scout, Invincible*
Don Army
Listed above, including several naval batteries distributed between the Don and Caucasian Armies and the 9th at Taganrog
Caucasian Army
1st Armored Train Battery: *Forward for Fatherland, United Russia, General Alexiev, Steppe*
Attached: Three Don trains
Northern Caucasus Forces
Kavkazets, Saint George Bringer of Victory, Terets
Trans-Caspian Forces
General Kornilov, Scout, Thunderstorm, Partisan, Three Musketeers

White armored train in Vladivostok, eastern Siberia. Naval guns have canvas muzzle covers for transportation. This is a mixed army-navy crew. Note plated demi-roof and hinged platforms in wagon sides. (National Archives)

Several trains were being equipped from September 1919 to early 1920 and these saw action only at the end of the campaign, mostly near Novorossisk as a mobile reserve: *To Moscow, For Holy Russia, Mighty, General Chernyaev, Apsheronets, White Seaman, Hurricane.*

White commanders created or captured additional armored trains which did not appear in the order of battle; for example, General Shkuro used his namesake train as his mobile headquarters.

Other trains and/or where they are known to have fought include:

General Gayman (previously the *Volunteer*), *Black Kite* and *Wolf* in the central Ukraine

Plastun, Bayan, General Dukhonin near Kiev

Glory of Kuban near Voronezh

Kazak and light armored train *Moscow* near Kursk

Mstislav the Bold at Kharkov

Cavalryman at Poltava

Colonel Zapolsky against Makhno in the Ukraine

Novorossiya near Odessa

Kavkazets, Dagestanets and *Shirvanets* in the north Caucasus

Zhelbat 1 (later *Student*), *Zhelbat 2, Falcon*, and the heavy armored train *Moscow* in the Crimea

Additional: *General Schifner-Markevich, Hero, General Skobelev*, and *Kuban Partisan*

In October *Officer* and *Ivan Kalita* supported the Kornilov Divizion's battles for Orel, the high water mark of the AFSR in the bid for Moscow. In one action, the two White trains engaged four Red counterparts and put the *International* out of action. Heavily outnumbered, the elite units were pushed out of Orel and an ensuing counter-attack at the end of the month failed to win back the city. After Budenny's *Konarmiya* defeated the Cossacks at Voronezh and Kastornaia, the armored trains fell back in the general retirement of the AFSR.

During the orderly retreat to Kursk and then Kharkov, the White trains fought to keep from being cut off by the regiments of harrying Red cavalry. Winter and typhus set in. Congestion on the railways became a virtual bottleneck north of Rostov, through which most of the White formations and a terrified civilian population attempted to retreat. The withdrawal had begun to assume the dimensions of a rout.

In the Ukraine, Red divisions outflanked the threadbare White units north of Kiev in November and both enemies moved south, the Whites trying to avoid being cut off from either Odessa or the Crimea. The Reds destroyed four armored trains and captured 15 near Odessa in February 1920.

White armored trains that survived the disastrous retreat through Rostov participated in battles along the southern Don and in the northern Kuban in January and February. As the AFSR fell back on Novorossisk, the trains fought rear-guard actions against both the Reds and Green partisans before being captured or sabotaged by their White crews. Cut-off from retreat, White trains in the Trans-Caspian and Northern Caucasian regions met similar ends.

Armored trains in Wrangel's Russian Army

General Slaschev directed several trains and tanks that had fallen back successfully to the Crimea to help secure the two entrances to the peninsula at Perekop and Taganach-Chongar in the early weeks of 1920. Under this defensive cover, the Whites were able to construct several new trains, using weapons that had been evacuated along with resources available in the Crimea. Naval guns were mounted on the *United Russia, Moscow* and *Ivan Kalita* to create heavy armored trains. Most of the new trains adopted the names of counterparts that had been lost in action. Veteran crews entered the new formations by 29 April:

1st Divizion: *General Alekseev, Sevastopol, United Russia*
2nd Divizion: *Glory of Kuban Officer, St. George Bringer of Victory, Grozny*
3rd Divizion: *Dmitry Don, Wolf, Ivan Kalita*
4th Divizion: *Soldier, Moscow, Drozdovtsi*
Don 3rd Corps trains (14 May): *Ataman Kaledin, Ataman Nazarov*

Armored trains participated with the tanks and armored cars as part of the combined-arms breakout in June. Wrangel's trains worked with the elite units to break Zhloba's Red cavalry in the Tauride that summer and advanced on the right flank with the Don Cossacks along the Sea of Azov. The armored trains covered the retreat during the Red offensive in October; *Soldier, Sevastopol, General Alekseev* and *Drozdovtsi* were captured or destroyed in actions from Alexandrovsk to Melitopol.

The remaining trains defended the entrances to the Crimea in the final days. Due to a freak change in the weather, the Reds were able to cross the Sivash shallows and outflank the White positions near Taganach while delivering a massed and costly frontal assault on the defenses at Perekop. Armored trains and cavalry covered the orderly withdrawal. Train crews fought their last actions as the White Army and civilian populace evacuated the Crimea by sea and at the last moment, sabotaged their trains. On 14 November *United Russia* and *St. George Bringer of Victory* were set on a direct collision course near Sevastopol.

COLORS AND MARKINGS OF WHITE ARMORED CARS AND TRAINS

Few troops in the field religiously followed the handful of official regulations governing the markings of armored units. Great variation occurred, but at the same time patterns that reflected traditions and commonly held values were maintained.

Base colors

Most White armored trains were painted dark olive, dark green, or gray, although instances of khaki and even black are not unknown. Kalmykov's train, the *Kalmykovets*, had one camouflaged command wagon as did at least one other photographed White train in the Trans-Caspian region (colors of both are unknown, but were possibly green and khaki). The majority of Russian armored cars had been painted dark olive during World War I, but during the Civil War dark green and gray also appeared. Pragmatically, White units tended to use stocks of paint on hand; thus, naval units

Cossack Ataman Kalmykov's command train, *Kalmykovets*, in Vladivostok, 1919–20. The center commander's wagon has two observation towers and eight machine-gun ports to a side. The pattern of color for the camouflaging is not known. (National Army Museum)

40

Artillery wagon of Cossack Ataman Kalmykov's command train, *Kalmykovets*, in Khabarovsk, eastern Siberia, American sector, 1919–20. The two guns with shields are accompanied by a larger gun to the right under tarpaulin covering. The wagon is "No. 1" (color probably black) and bears the Kalmykov emblem on the side, a black letter K against a yellow background. A yellow stripe may appear across the lower portion of the wagon side, or this may be merely an area shaded by the sun. Entry is by ladder and a curved sun-roof offers minor weather protection for crew and sensitive equipment. The *Kalmykovets* also carried a "Wagon of Death" where some of his more brutal executions took place. (National Archives)

outfitting armored trains and cars tended to use the color gray, while army units normally employed a shade of green or even khaki.

Names
Names on armored cars were in white on the side and additionally, though not always, on the armored plate just above the driver in front. Those of armored trains generally appeared in white, but sometimes in black, on the sides of wagons and/or in the front and rear.

National flag
The Russian tricolor of red, blue and white dated to the time of Tsar Peter the Great (red for the people, blue for the Tsar and white for God). Tricolor flags were flown from the tops of armored car or train turrets, or tied to the front of a car or on the side of the train's command wagon.

National roundel
Three colors in a circle, white, blue and red (from outer ring to inner) were painted on the sides of armored cars and trains.

National chevron
The Volunteer Army used the popular tricolor chevron before Denikin made it official for the AFSR in April 1919. This appeared on the sides of armored cars and command vehicles, armored trains and troop trains. In April 1920 Wrangel made the roundel official and eliminated the chevron in the new Russian Army.

Improvisations
Sometimes those who designed or built armored cars and trains improvised their own markings. White AFSR cavalry veteran Nicholas Volkov-Mouromtsoff witnessed two gray armored cars carrying the inscription *Chernomorski Flot* ("Black Sea Fleet") in white below the chevron.

The Cossacks
The Kuban Cossacks received nearly all their armored cars and perhaps all but four of their armored trains from the Russians: these were delivered with Volunteer Army and AFSR markings. The Don Cossacks employed a traditional heraldic symbol from May 1918, a black triangle on a yellow disc, itself bordered by a black line. This symbolized the concept of an arrowhead and wounded stag. The roundel appeared on the sides of armored cars and trains and sometimes on the front of cars below the driver's window. Their tricolor flag represented those peoples living within Don territory: scarlet for non-Cossacks, yellow for the Kalmucks and blue for the Don Cossacks. These flags could be seen attached to the right front of their armored cars as well as affixed on the wagons of their armored trains. Once the Don entered the AFSR, Russian roundels and occasional chevrons were added even as the previous symbols were retained.

The Czechs
The Legion used the white over red flag of Czechoslovakia, born in

October 1918. White over red stripes appeared on the turrets and sides of armored cars as ⅔ white and ⅓ red. The armored car *Adski* bore a white skull and crossbones on its single turret in 1918, while the *Grozny* had a base color of dark green, the name in yellow. The sides of Czech trains often displayed colorful representations of fairy tales, floral designs and pastoral scenes reminiscent of the home country.

COLORS AND MARKINGS OF WHITE TANKS

British tanks arrived in Russia painted dark green; however, recent research at the Tank Museum indicates that many of those coming directly from France would have been khaki brown. Wrangel had one detachment of tanks in "protective color" according to one White veteran. British tanks bore Royal Tank Corps identification stripes of white-red-white placed vertically on the front sides or horns. Photos also depict the Whippets with vertical red-white-red-white-red stripes on the front and rear lower sloping plates. This pattern apparently deviated from official Tank Corps charts.

Russian tricolor roundels were painted on the cabs of the Whippets, especially under Wrangel. Denikin does not seem to have employed either the roundel or chevron, but sometimes painted the Russian tricolor horizontally on the horns of the Mark V. Wrangel continued this horizontal scheme. The Northwest Army painted this tricolor flag vertically in the same position.

Names
British personnel unofficially named their tanks in white, either on the side, as in the Whippet *Love Child* photographed in the Kuban, or on the front sloping plate of a Mark V, as in the *Captain Cromie*. This latter tank additionally had two crossed flags, a British Union Jack flag and a St. Andrew's flag painted above its name. The Whites named their tanks in white or black, the names appearing on the front plate or front sides of a Mark V or on the sides of the cab of a Whippet.

BIBLIOGRAPHY

The authors believe this is the first book on the Russian Civil War that brings together the triad of armored components: armored cars, tanks and armored trains. Historians inside Russia have produced at least four serious works on Russian Civil War armor during the last five years. Two of these books dealt with armored cars, one covered tanks, and one delved into armored trains. Despite this recent activity, color renderings of White Army armored trains are not believed to have existed before the publication of this Osprey volume.

Material about the armored units of the Red Army is more readily available, of course, than

Armored train *General Shkuro*, named for General Andrei Grigorevich Shkuro of the elite "White Wolves" Kuban Cossacks. According to Major Williamson, artillery inspector attached to the British Military Mission, Shkuro's command train had a pack of wolves pursuing prey painted on the side. The insignia on the center of this wagon appears to have a wolf's head facing right and surmounting two crossed flags, colors unknown. The Reds captured this train in November 1919, during the massed cavalry battles near Kastornaia and Voronezh. (Kolomiets)

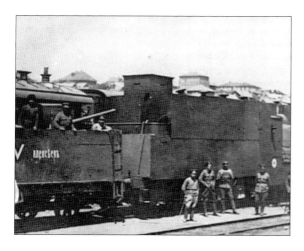

Light armored train *General Alekseev*, southern front, 1919. Named after General Mikhail Vasilevich Alekseev, former chief-of-staff, Imperial Russian Army, and former chief-of-staff, Volunteer Army. Originally captured from the Reds during the second Kuban campaign, summer 1918, the train received its name after the death of Alekseev in November 1918. Initially armed with a 3-in. gun and one machine-gun wagon, the *General Alekseev* had been upgraded to two guns by January 1919. The train supported General Baron Wrangel's Caucasian Army as part of the 1st Armored Train Battery in the attack on and defense of Tsaritsyn. While attached to the 4th Armored Train Battery, the *General Alekseev* saw distinguished service in the Crimea and northern Tauride until the Reds finally put the train out of action near Sokologornaia in late October 1920. The tri-color roundel to the right appears in white-blue-red from outer circle to inner. Note chevron at left. (Kolomiets)

material about their enemies, the Whites. Defeated, the Whites had to destroy or abandon their armored units. Captured White tanks, armored trains and armored cars were either adapted for use in the Red Army, cannibalized for parts, or were simply sent to scrap heaps to perish in the graveyard of history.

Therefore, the research behind this Osprey volume has involved many people from many countries, both alive and deceased, from White combatants and émigrés, to Red veterans and historians, to Allied participants. Our research has involved a synthesis of old and new works along with photographic evidence going backmore than 80 years.

The following bibliography can only suggest a few of the works we have used.

Works in Russian

Baryatinsky, M., Kolomiets, M., *Armored Cars of the Russian Army, 1906–1917* (Moscow, 2000).

Baryatinsky, M., Kolomiets, M., *Austin Armored Car* (Moscow, 1997).

Deryabin, A.I., *Civil War in Russia: National Armies* (Moscow, 1998).

Deryabin, A.I., *Civil War in Russia: Armies of the Interventionists* (Moscow, 1998).

Drogovaz, I.G. *Fortress on Wheels: the History of Armored Trains* (Minsk, 2002).

Encyclopedia of the Civil War and Military Intervention in the USSR (Moscow, 1983).

Kolomiets, M., Moshchansky, E., and Romadin, S., *Tanks of the Civil War* (Moscow, 1999).

Raykhtsaum, A.L., *Use of Tanks in Wrangel's Army*, Domestic Archives, No. 6 (Moscow, 1992).

White Guard Almanac, No. 3 (Moscow, 1999–2000).

White Guard Almanac, No. 5 (Moscow, 2001).

Wolves, S.V., *White Movement in Russia: Organizational Structure* (Moscow, 2000).

Works in English and French

Bryan, J., "With the Tanks in North Russia," *Tank Corps Journal*, Vol. 1 (Bournemouth, 1919–20).

Fletcher, D., *The British Tanks, 1915–1919* (Ramsbury, 2001).

Fuller, J.F.C. (believed to be author), "A Visit to the South Russian Tank Corps, July to October 1919," *Tank Corps Journal*, Vol. 1 (Bournemouth, 1919–20).

Hope-Carson, E., "British Tanks in Northwest Russia," *Tank Corps Journal*, Vols. 8–9 (Bournemouth, 1926–28).

Kudlicka, B., "Orlik: Armored Train of the Czechoslovak Legion in Russia," *Tankograd Gazette* (unknown).

Malmassari, P., *Armored Trains, 1826–1989* (Editions Heimdahl, 1989).

Williamson, H., *Farewell to the Don* (New York, 1971).

Wreden, N., *The Unmaking of a Russian* (New York, 1935).

COLOR PLATE COMMENTARY

A1: DON COSSACK ARMORED CAR *MEDVEDITSA*, SUMMER 1919

This car was named in honor of the village of Ust-Medved-itskaia, which rose against the Reds in spring 1919. This Austin first series was rebuilt on a truck chassis, hence the solid double tire configuration on the rear axles. Solid rubber bulletproof Russian Gusmatik tires were installed on the front axles and the front mudguards were removed. Russian modifications included machine-gun shields, the driver's door and the folding plate in the front of the driver. The yellow circle, black triangle and border represent the Don Army, while the tricolor roundel indicates subordination to the Armed Forces of South Russia (AFSR). The flag of the Don Cossacks, scarlet, yellow and blue, is attached to the front.

A2: VOLUNTEER ARMY ARMORED CAR *MIGHTY*, 1919

The Austin third series normally sported double rear wheels; however, the White Army tended to remove these as spares. The name in the inset above is *Brave*. These armored cars arrived from Britain new, in dark green, at the port of Novorossisk in April 1919. Along with their sister car *Vigilant*, they formed the 2nd Armored Car Detachment assigned to the Caucasian Army, AFSR. The roundel and chevron appeared in the Russian national colors of red, blue and white. The Whites often used flags on their armored cars in order to better identify themselves from their various opponents.

B1: RENAULT FT-17 TANK, 1920

This Reno is one of two belonging to the Detached Platoon, 1st Tank Division, Crimea, summer 1920. The two tanks were named *Modest* and *Gray* but the color of the names and exact positions are not known. This light tank bears the tricolor roundels of Baron Wrangel's Russian Army, and

Machine-gun wagon of *United Russia*, Southern Front. Note Volunteer Army chevron on side (red-blue-white) from bottom to top and the Russian tricolor flag to the right. On the top of the wagon are two machine-gun turrets and commander's turret. Note machine-gun shields and older cyrillic letters in white. (Kolomiets)

remains in the original French beige, green and brown camouflage. These tanks were initially part of the French armored force at Odessa, spring 1919, and had been assigned to the 303rd Company, 1st Battalion, 501st Special Artillery Regiment (some confusion about the actual unit subordination has occurred in previous historical records).

B2: MEDIUM MARK A WHIPPET TANK *SPHINX*, 1920

Tank No. A371 *Sphinx* is shown here just prior to capture by Red forces at the Kakhovka bridgehead, 5 September 1920. As part of the 2nd Tank Detachment, 1st Tank Division, *Sphinx* cleared the barbed wire entanglements before being knocked out by Red artillery. Note the British Tank Corps identification stripes and Russian tricolor roundel. All Whippets sent to Russia had their serial numbers, beginning with the white alpha character A, followed by three digits, starting either with 2 or 3, painted on their cabs.

C1: MARK V TANK NO. 9261 *FIRST AID*, NORTHWEST RUSSIA, 1919

Six Mark V composite tanks of the Northwest Russian Tank Detachment assembled in Estonia in August 1919 to support General N.N. Yudenich's White Northwestern Army. After inspecting the tanks, Yudenich christened No. 9261 *First Aid*. British Captain L.H. Battersby initially commanded *First Aid* until being succeeded for the final actions by a Russian naval officer, Commander Bystrumov. In this plate the tank bears

Artillery wagon of *United Russia*, Southern Front. Note Volunteer Army chevrons on the side and newer cyrillic letters at right in white.

the red, blue and white tricolor vertically according to procedures established by the Northwestern Army. All Mark Vs sent to Russia had four white numbers starting with "9" on the side and to the rear of the sponson.

C2: MEDIUM MARK B TANK, NO. 1613, NORTH RUSSIA, 1919

The North Russian Tank Detachment arrived in the White Sea port of Archangel in August 1919. Two Medium Mark B tanks landed, including No. 1613. Medium Bs sent to Russia had four white numerals on the side, slightly to the rear of center. The British left two tanks behind for the local White forces when they evacuated in October 1919, a Mark V and No. 1613. General Miller's Whites sank the tanks in the North Dvina River in February 1920 in order to avoid their capture; nevertheless, the Reds recovered No. 1613 and sent it to Moscow. No. 1613 entered the Red Army painted in camouflage and with hammer and plough symbols superimposed on a red star on the cab.

D: MARK V COMPOSITE TANK NO. 9358, *FOR HOLY RUSSIA*, KAKHOVKA, AUTUMN 1920

For Holy Russia served in the 3rd Tank Detachment, 1st Tank Divizion, in General Baron Wrangel's Russian Army in 1920. This tank was a composite Mark V, which consisted of one "male" sponson (6-pdr gun and one machine gun), one female sponson (two machine guns), and one machine gun in the front and one in the rear. All Mark V tanks sent to Russia seem to have been composites except for two "females" that only housed machine guns.

Mark V tanks essentially followed the internal layout of the earlier Mark IV. However, the new design included several alterations: better observation points, additional ventilation, a new and more powerful engine, an additional rear hatch and door, improved track cleaning, more convenient storage, superior maneuvering capabilities and new one-driver control.

The tank's interior featured walls painted in gloss white and a floor painted in light gray. Many sub-components retained their original metallic finishes. Externally, the tank remained in the British dark olive green. The Whites painted the Russian national tricolor horizontally over the original

Don Cossack armored train *Azovets*, attached to the 1st Armored Railway Regiment, Don Armored Train Brigade, southern front. The *Azovets* participated in fierce fighting around Voronezh in September 1919. During the retreat, the Cossacks drove the train into the River Don to prevent capture. (Kolomiets)

White armored train, Rostov-on-Don, 1919. Sources indicate this train may be either the *General Drozdovsky*, or a Don Cossack train. The lettering, apparently in black along the side of the first wagon, is indecipherable. (Kolomiets)

British identification colors of white and red. The Whites painted the tank's name in white on the front sloping plate below the front cab and retained the tank's number in white on the side and to the rear of the sponson (see insets).

For Holy Russia penetrated deep into the Red defenses at Kakhovka in October 1920 before being struck in the left side by artillery. Red captors cannibalized parts from other Mark Vs taken in action in order to repair the tank and subsequently renamed it the Muscovite Proletarian.

E1: CZECH ARMORED MOTOR WAGON *ZAAMUREC*, SIBERIA 1919–20

The Czech Legion captured Red armored train No. 4, *Polupanov*, in Simbirsk on 22 July 1918. This train consisted of the *Zaamurec* motor wagon, two artillery wagons, an armored locomotive and a tender. The Czechs renamed this armored train *Orlik* or "Young Eagle." *Zaamurec* had been designed in 1916 on a Fax-Arbel flatbed, with walls of 16mm (0.63in.) armor (12mm/0.47in. on sloped sections) and two Italian 60-hp petrol engines. Each turret could rotate 360 degrees and the guns could fire 10 degrees downward and 60 degrees upward. Fire control turrets were added in 1917. *Zaamurec* carried eight machine guns, eight periscopes, an intercom system, signaling equipment, two searchlights and two artillery range finders. The original 57mm Nordenfeld guns were changed to 76.2mm weapons in 1918. The name *Orlik* appeared in white, machine-metaled letters that were bolted onto the right side of the front turret; thus, in this depiction, the letters would appear on the opposite side. The letters vuz cis. 1, mean "wagon number 1." *Zaamurec* could operate as part of the *Orlik* configuration, or independently.

E2: CZECH ARMORED TRAIN *ORLIK*, CENTRAL SIBERIA, 1919–20

This plate depicts the usual components of *Orlik*, exclusive of the *Zaamurec* motor wagon. The first Czech national flag of white and red appears in the inset. *Orlik* had a "ChN" type armored locomotive with 12mm (0.47in.) steel plating, that burned either coal or wood. The *Orlik* echelon or configuration included two double-axle artillery wagons with similar profiles, each mounting 12 machine guns. The first, with a conical gun turret, carried a 76.2mm Model 1902 piece, while the second, with a cylindrical turret, sported a mountain gun, 76.2mm Model 1904. The turrets could traverse 270 degrees. The crew of 100 included four officers. The train roamed the length of the Trans-Siberian, clearing away Red and Green partisans until the Czech evacuation from Vladivostok in May 1920. Thereafter, *Orlik* served the remnants of the White Army operating in the Russian Far East. After Vladivostok fell to the Reds in 1922, the Whites moved the train to Manchuria where it served a local Chinese warlord for six years before vanishing from history.

F1: VOLUNTEER ARMY ARMORED TRAIN *FORWARD FOR FATHERLAND*, SUMMER 1918

Established on 14 July 1918 at Tikhoretskaia, after being captured from the Reds, the train's composition included an armored "Ov" type locomotive and armored tender, a half-armored wagon with a 75mm piece, a machine-gun wagon with eight machine guns (not shown here) and an armored wagon with a 3-in. gun. The name appeared in white on the side of the engine. The double-headed eagle emblem of the Romanovs can be seen in white on the side of the 3-in. gun wagon. This train participated in the second Kuban campaign, the clearing of the northern Caucasus and subsequently served in the Caucasian Army, AFSR.

F2: VOLUNTEER ARMY, ARMORED TRAIN *OFFICER*, FEBRUARY 1919

The Whites captured *Officer* in August 1918. The crew numbered 48 officers and 67 enlisted men. Abandoned at Novorossisk in March 1920, the train configuration and crew re-emerged in the Crimea as the *Glory of Kuban* in April.

Officer comprised two identical double-axle armored gun wagons that housed 76.2mm Model 1902 field pieces with a 360-degree traverse, an armored "Ch" type locomotive, and a tender that contained the commander's compartment and two machine guns. The casement of the armored gun wagons sported 12 Maxim machine guns, five per side and

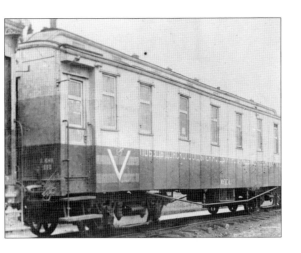

Don Cossack train, south Russia, 1919. The white letters along the side read "Train of Don Propaganda Section… " before becoming indecipherable. The emblem left of center is on all train wagons. The field of the emblem alternates black and orange, colors of the Order of St. George, given for heroism. Superimposed on the field at the top is a silver sword piercing a silver crown of thorns, an heroic symbol of sacrifice adopted by the Volunteer Army and Don Cossacks who had participated in the "Ice March" in the Kuban during 1918. The chevron from bottom to top is red, blue and white. (Deryabin)

an additional pair capable of firing forward from the front of each wagon.

The enlarged portion of this plate reveals machine-gun ports, the double-headed Imperial eagle in white, and the tricolor roundel. The Volunteer Army painted *Officer* in white lettering on both sides of each gun wagon as well as at the front of each turret.

G1: VOLUNTEER ARMY ARMORED TRAIN *TO MOSCOW*, WINTER 1919–SPRING 1920

Established 13 September 1919 at the Sudostal Works, Novorossisk, the heavy armored train *To Moscow* defended the Rostov–Novorossisk sector until being captured by the

Reds in March 1920. The echelon consisted of two almost identical gun wagons (each with two machine guns in sponsons on the side), at least one machine-gun wagon and an engine and tender. The gun wagons had the black lettering (with red shading behind the black) *To Moscow* superimposed on the side and front over Volunteer Army chevrons. The black double-headed eagle symbolizes Russia's claim to be the Third Rome after the fall of the Byzantine Empire and is seen here without the crown, orb and scepter of the Romanov Dynasty. The flag bears the Russian tricolor in the upper corner and also the symbol of the armored train service, that of crossed cannon barrels and a winged wheel on rails. Black numbers 9 49922 and 9 48878 appeared to the front of the gun wagons. According to Russian sources, the guns were 107mm or 122mm weapons; however, the gun on this wagon appears to be a remounted British 60-pdr. The train itself appears in heavily weathered khaki.

G2: WHITE SIBERIAN ARMORED TRAIN *VITYAZ*, FALL 1920

Established in spring 1920, *Vityaz* or "Knight" had a complement of 100 officers and 35 enlisted men, commanded by Colonel F.F. Meibom. All were select volunteers from the late General V.O. Kappel's Volga Brigade. *Vityaz* fought in eastern Siberia and in one encounter destroyed the Red armored train *Comrade Blyukher*.

This train consisted of an armored locomotive and tender, two armored wagons, two semi-armored wagon platforms with guns and two wagon platforms carrying engineering material. The six guns included one naval Canet, a 4.5-in. howitzer, one 47mm Hotchkiss on the tower next to the commander and three 3-in. Japanese field pieces. Ten Maxim and eight Colt machine guns bristled along the casements of the armored wagons. The armored train's name in white was superimposed above the white lettering "For Rus, Sacred, United and Indivisible." Above the commander's position flew the Russian national flag.

Kuban Cossack armored train No. 4, constructed by the Kuban Railway Sotnia. The letters, crossed axe, and anchor are white. Note the well-armored locomotive. (Kolomiets)

INDEX